江苏省高校优势学科建设工程项目资助
江苏省高校品牌专业建设工程资助项目

Chinese Wushu English Teaching
中国武术英语教程

张宗豪　王　平　**主　编**
刘卫东　朱扬涛　**副主编**

苏州大学出版社

图书在版编目(CIP)数据

中国武术英语教程 = Chinese Wushu English Teaching / 张宗豪,王平主编. —苏州:苏州大学出版社,2019.3（2023.8 重印）
江苏省高校优势学科建设工程项目资助　江苏省高校品牌专业建设工程资助项目
ISBN 978-7-5672-2412-4

Ⅰ.①中… Ⅱ.①张… ②王… Ⅲ.①武术－中国－英语－高等学校－教材 Ⅳ.①G852

中国版本图书馆 CIP 数据核字(2018)第 114820 号

Chinese Wushu English Teaching
中国武术英语教程
张宗豪　王　平　主编
责任编辑　金莉莉

苏州大学出版社出版发行
(地址:苏州市十梓街 1 号　邮编:215006)
广东虎彩云印刷有限公司印装
(地址:东莞市虎门镇黄村社区厚虎路 20 号 C 幢一楼　邮编:523898)

开本 700 mm×1 000 mm　1/16　印张 9.5　字数 161 千
2019 年 3 月第 1 版　2023 年 8 月第 3 次印刷
ISBN 978-7-5672-2412-4　定价:30.00 元

苏州大学版图书若有印装错误,本社负责调换
苏州大学出版社营销部　电话:0512 -67481020
苏州大学出版社网址　http://www.sudapress.com
苏州大学出版社邮箱　sdcbs@suda.edu.cn

前言

中华武术博大精深,深受世界各国武术爱好者的喜爱。其丰富的中国传统文化思想让外国友人情有独钟,越来越多的国外武术爱好者加入了练习中国武术、探索中国优秀文化的队伍中来。然而,武术独特的民族性、国与国之间的文化差异性、语言交流的困难性在很大程度上制约了武术的传播与发展。在武术教学中外国人很难真正理解武术的内涵,如何使用地道的英语口语,进行原汁原味的武术教学就显得尤为重要。

本人曾作为访问学者赴美国MD安德森癌症中心进行为期一年的太极拳方面的实验研究,同时从事武术特别是太极拳的教学工作。在教学过程中,本人发现了一个非常棘手的问题,就是在教授武术套路和相关武术文化的过程中,美国学生有时候不能够理解老师自认为已经表达清楚的内容,和他们沟通的时候他们指出了本人在英语表达上存在的问题。基于此,本人在美国的许多武术爱好者及英语专家Elizabeth女士的帮助下参与编写了《太极英语》一书,该书获得了良好的反响。在此基础上作为《太极英语》姊妹篇的《中国武术英语教程》也应运而生,本人希望能为更好地向世界传播武术、弘扬中国传统文化尽一份绵薄之力。

本书的一部分内容参考了目前国内外一些有关武术的图书,如《汉英——英汉武术气功词汇》《英汉汉英武术常用词汇》等,同时我们对部分词汇及其翻译进行了筛选;另一部分内容则是我们在国外武术教学过程中通过现场交流而翻译的。本书共分为武术文化介绍、武术课堂英语、武术套路英语教学、武术套路名称、一般词汇、武术专业词汇六个部分。为了便于读者记忆,本书有两点说明:(1)除套路动作名称及某些专业术语的首字母大写外,其他词条一般均小写。(2)为简洁起见,一些词条(如套路动作名称)的译文一般省略其中的冠词和代词,而一些基本词汇，如武术基本功、器械技法名称等中的冠词或代词则予以保留。

在本书撰写的过程中，本人得到了美国英语专家 Elizabeth 女士、美国休斯敦少林武术学院院长释行浩先生和苏州大学体育学院王国志教授、刘卫东博士、王平副教授的大力支持，正是他们的无私奉献和帮助才促成了本书的撰写。同时，本人在编写过程中也参考了许多专家编写的资料和图书，在此表示深深的谢意！

由于本人从事英文翻译工作不久，翻译难免有不足之处，书中存在一些疏漏和缺憾，恳请国内外的专家、读者不吝指正。

最后，本人真诚地祝愿中国武术的发展有一个更加光辉灿烂的明天！

张宗豪

2018 年 11 月 8 日于苏州大学

目 录

CHAPTER 1 WUSHU CULTURE INTRODUCTION
第一章 武术文化介绍 ………………………………… 001

CHAPTER 2 WUSHU CLASSROOM ENGLISH
第二章 武术课堂英语 ………………………………… 023

CHAPTER 3 WUSHU ROUTINE ENGLISH TEACHING
第三章 武术套路英语教学 …………………………… 041

CHAPTER 4 NAMES OF WUSHU ROUTINE
第四章 武术套路名称 ………………………………… 063

CHAPTER 5 GENERAL VOCABULARY
第五章 一般词汇 ……………………………………… 075

CHAPTER 6 WUSHU SPECIFIC WORDS
第六章 武术专业词汇 ………………………………… 119

参考文献 ………………………………………………… 146

第一章
CHAPTER 1

武术文化介绍

WUSHU CULTURE INTRODUCTION

1. 当前,武术的概念界定为:"武术是以技击动作为主要内容,以套路、格斗和功法练习为活动形式,注重内外兼修的中国传统体育项目。"

Nowadays, Wushu is generally defined as "a tradition Chinese sport focusing on the cultivation of physical health and spiritual power, and with combative movements as the main contents, and with taolu(routine), gedou (fighting) and gongfa (training skills) as the form of practice".

2. 中国武术将踢、打、摔、拿、击、刺等技击动作为素材,遵照攻守进退、动静疾徐、刚柔虚实等规律组成套路,以此来增强体质、培养意志、训练格斗技能。

Chinese Wushu takes kicking, punching, throwing, controlling, hitting, thrusting and other combative movements as its basic elements to strengthen the physique, cultivate the will, and train gedou skills.

3. 中国武术按其价值功能可分为攻防技击类武术、艺术表现类武术和健身养生类武术。其运动形式有套路、搏斗、功力、养生等。

Chinese Wushu can be functionally divided into combative Wushu, artistic expression Wushu and fitness and health-keeping Wushu. Sports forms include routine, combating, skill, fitness building and so on.

4. 套路运动有中国拳术、器械、对练、集体演练等运动形式。

Routine is in the form of Chinese boxing, weapon, sparring, group drilling and so on.

5. 武术套路作为中国武术特有的表现形式之一,具有三个特点:一是民族性,二是技击性,三是艺术性。

Wushu routine, as one of the unique forms of Chinese Wushu, bears the following three features: nationality, attacking and artistry.

6. 中国武术有着悠久的历史,它最初是中华民族的先民在与自然和社会环境进行斗争的过程中萌生出的一种本能的个体技击能力。

Chinese Wushu has a long history. Originally as an individual combative skill, it was developed by Chinese ancestors in their struggle against natural and social environments to survive.

7. 中国武术体现出习武者的精、气、神,具有独特的民族精神和文化底蕴。

Chinese Wushu embodies the practitioners' essence, breath and spirit, with unique spirit and cultural deposits.

8. 中国武术已经成为中华民族文化的象征,尤其是它的包容性更增添了其神秘感。

Chinese Wushu has become a token of Chinese culture, and especially its inclusiveness helps add a sense of mystery to it.

9. 时至今日,中国武术已自成体系,不仅具有强身健体的作用,还有防身自卫的功能及其特有的审美价值,深受人们喜爱。

Up to now, Chinese Wushu has established a system of its own. It is very popular not only as an exercise for body fitness, but also for its function of self-defense and its distinctive aesthetic value.

10. 武术是一种文化现象,它的形成与物质文明、精神文明的发展紧密相关,是人们在生产劳动和军事生活中逐渐形成的对社会观念、信仰的反映。

Wushu is a cultural phenomenon. It evolves alongside the developement of material and spiritual civilizations and mirrors social concepts and beliefs as they are gradually formed in people's work and military life.

11. 作为一个整体意义上的文化形态,中国武术根植于中国传统文化之中。

As a cultural form in a whole sense, Chinese Wushu is rooted in the traditional Chinese culture.

12. 今天,中国武术已经成为沟通中国和世界的友谊桥梁及传递友谊的纽带,成为世界更好了解中国的一个窗口。

Today Chinese Wushu has become a bridge of friendship linking China and the world and a bond of transferring friendship, and has served as a window through which the world can gain better understanding of China.

13. 尤其是近 30 年来,中国武术已经发生了质的变化,已经完成了体育化、竞技化和国际化的改革。

Especially in the last three decades, significant progress has been made to transform Chinese Wushu into competitive sports and to popularize it on an international level.

14. 在不同的历史时期,人们对武术的需求和认识不尽相同。

During different historical periods, people had different needs and perceptions of Wushu.

15. 武术的内容、形式和价值功能的不断变化,以及不同的社会环境和认知水平差异等因素的存在，使得人们在对武术的概念定义时也出现了不同的表述。

Due to the constant change of content, form and value function of Wushu and the existence of factors like different social environments and people's cognitive levels, people have different expressions for the concept of Wushu.

16. 中国武术一向"尚武崇德"，重礼仪，讲道德。

Chinese Wushu has put great emphasis on the promotion of etiquette and morality.

17. 武术谚语有"未曾学艺先学礼，未曾习武先习德"，充分显示了武德教化在武术传授过程中所表现出的道德上的文化特征。

As a Wushu proverb goes, "Learn morality before Wushu is ever learned, and acquire virtues before Wushu is ever acquired." It shows that it is inherent in Wushu that Wushu ethics is placed at a central position in Wushu training.

18. 中国武术始终把武德列为习武的先决条件。

Wushu ethics is the precondition to regulate practitioners' behavior.

19. 可见武德是中国历代习武者的共同信仰和精神价值取向。

It is obvious that Wushu ethics is common faith and spiritual value orientation shared by Chinese Wushu practitioners from generation to generation.

20. 武德在长期的历史积淀、传承之中已经同人们的生活方式、思维模式、行为准则、道德情操、审美情趣、处世态度和风俗习惯融为一体，成为中华民族伦理道德的重要组成部分。

In the long history of precipitation and inheritance, Wushu ethics has fused with people's lifestyle, mode of thinking, code of conduct, moral sentiment, aesthetic taste, attitude towards life, custom and habit. It has become an important integral part of Chinese ethics.

21. 武术动作具有攻防技击性，它的技术来源于技击实践。

Wushu movements are characterized by attacking and defending. The skills come from its real combating.

22. 武术正是具备了这样的特点和本质属性，才得以区别其他体育项目。

Characteristics and essential attributes of Wushu distinguish it from other sports.

23. 武术的技击特点使武术形成了自己的完整技术体系。

Combative characteristics of Wushu enable it to form a complete skill system of its own.

24. 作为中国武术特有的表现形式的武术套路,虽然拳种不同,风格各异,但都是以踢、打、摔、拿、击、刺等攻防技击动作构成套路的主要内容。

Routine, as a special form of Chinese Wushu, includes different sorts and styles, but all the sorts are in common in terms of combative movements for attacking and defending, such as kicking, punching, throwing, controlling, hitting, thrusting and so on.

25. 表现攻与防的内在含义与精神是套路技术的核心。

The core of routine skills is to demonstrate the inner meaning and spirit of attacking and defending.

26. 随着武术技术的发展,武术的本质特征——技击性有所减弱,但其仍将作为武术技术根本的特点长期存在。

With the development of Wushu skills, the essential characteristic of Wushu (attacking) has been weakened, but it will still exist in the long run as the fundamental feature of Wushu skills.

27. 中国传统文化的最高价值原则是和谐统一,既讲究动作的形体规范,又要求精气神传意、内外合一的整体运动观,这是中国武术的一大特点。

The highest value principle of Chinese traditional culture lies in harmony and unity. Chinese Wushu emphasizes both standardized movements and the unity of body and spirit, which is one of the characteristics of Chinese Wushu.

28. 注重个人身心动作的和谐,强调"内三合"和"外三合",关于内外相合的理论在武术不同拳种中都曾有所提及,可以认为它是中国武术各拳种的一个共同要求。

The harmony of body and mind is a common requirement of various sorts of Chinese Wushu. The theories of Three Internal Harmonies and Three External Harmonies have been mentioned in different sorts of Quan.

29. 所谓内,指人的精神、意识和气息的运行;所谓外,指人的手、眼、身、法、步的形体活动。

The "internal" refers to the circulation of spirit, consciousness and breath; the "external" means movements of hands, eyes, body, skills, steps.

30. 不论是哪种拳种,套路在技术上都特别要求把内在的精气神与外在的形体动作紧密结合。

Regardless of any sort of Quan, routine technically requires a close combination of the inner spirit and the external body movements.

31. 这一特点充分体现了武术作为一种文化形式,在长期的历史发展中备受中国古代哲学、医学、美学等方面的影响。

It fully reflects the fact that Wushu, as a cultural form, has been affected by ancient Chinese philosophy, medicine, aesthetics, etc. during its long-term development.

32. 形神问题不仅是一个技术问题,还是中国传统文化特点在武术运动中的集中体现。

The unity of body and spirit is not only an issue of skills, but also epitomizes Chinese traditional culture in the form of Wushu.

33. 武术的内容丰富,形式多样,分别适应不同年龄、性别、职业、体质的人的需要,人们可以根据自己的条件和兴趣加以选择。

Wushu is rich in content and it has many forms. It is suitable for people of different ages, genders, professions and health conditions respectively, and it is optional according to individual conditions and interests.

34. 武术运动不受时间、季节、场地器材的限制,这给开展群众性体育活动创造了有利的条件。

Wushu is not restricted by time, season and facilities, which creates a favourable condition for people to practise Wushu.

35. 这些武术动作对人体的反应速度、力量、灵巧、耐力等都有良好的促进作用。

These Wushu movements are beneficial to reaction velocity, strength, agility and endurance of human body.

36. 不同的人可以根据个人的不同要求选择适合自己的项目进行练习,从而发挥武术的健身作用,达到增强体质的目的。

Different people can choose certain routine or Wushu styles according to their individual different requirements so as to play the role of Wushu fitness and achieve the purpose of strengthening the physique.

37. 在武术创立之初,防身自卫就是其根本的目的。

Self-defence is Wushu's fundamental purpose since it came into being.

38. 到了现代社会,武术的技击价值虽然已不是很突出,但由于我们在日常生活中还是会遇到一些危及自身和他人安全的情况,所以武术的技击价值依然不容忽视。

Even though Wushu's combative value has become less prominent in modern society, it can not be ignored since it is still possible that our personal safety and that of the others may be endangered in our daily life.

39. 现今的搏斗运动虽然属于体育范畴,但其技术方法与实用技击术十分接近,绝大多数技术动作在实际搏斗中可直接运用。

The current fighting is classified as physical exercise, but the technical skills are quite close to practical combat and most technical actions can be directly applied in real fight.

40. 人们可以通过套路动作练习掌握防身自卫的知识和方法,同时也可以提高必要的身体素质和对意外情况的应变能力。

Through routine movement exercise, people may have command of knowledge and methods of self-defense and meanwhile may strengthen necessary physical quality and the ability to cope with unexpected incidents.

41. "未曾习武先习德"说明武术练习历来十分重视武德教育。

"Acquire virtues before Wushu is ever acquired" indicates that Wushu ethnics education has always been emphasized during Wushu exercise.

42. 武德可以理解为习武之人应具备的道德,是习武者把握社会、实现社会价值而建立的自我约束与自律精神体系。

Wushu ethnics can be understood as the virtue that Wushu practitioners are required to have. It refers to the spiritual system of self-control and self-discipline established by Wushu practitioners for the purpose of grasping society and realizing social value.

43. 很显然武术在娱乐身心、增强交流及传播中国传统文化方面都具有非常重要的作用。

It is obvious that Wushu plays an important role in entertaining body and soul, strengthening communication and exchanging Chinese traditional culture.

44. 同时,武术的练习过程需要吃苦耐劳和坚持不懈的精神。

Meanwhile, the exercise process of Wushu requires the spirit of endurance of hard work and perseverance.

45. 中国政府一直不断地向国外派出武术队,积极开展武术国际交流和推广活动。

Chinese government has been sending Wushu teams to other countries constantly to actively carry out international exchange and promotion activities of Wushu.

46. 自中华人民共和国成立以来,武术在学校教育中的作用越来越重要,在开展校园体育活动、丰富校园文化生活、增强学生体质方面都做出了很大的贡献。

Since the establishment of the People's Republic of China, Wushu has been playing a more and more important role in school education and has made a great contribution to developing campus physical activities, enriching campus culture and enhancing students' physique.

47. 武术具有很高的观赏价值。

Wushu has high ornamental value.

48. 各种武术活动,包括各种表演、比赛、训练等,都是以精神产品的形式为社会提供服务的。

All kinds of Wushu activities including various performances, competitions and trainings serve the society in the form of spiritual products.

49. 通过习武的共同爱好,特别是随着我国的改革开放,国家间的交流越来越频繁。

Through the common interest of Wushu practice, especially the Reform and Opening-up Policy of our country, the contact between countries becomes more and more frequent.

50. 这不仅有益于培养坚韧不拔、自强不息的意志,也是一种修身养性的重要手段,有益于人的全面发展。

It is not only beneficial to the cultivation of indomitableness and unremitting will, but also is an important way of morality cultivation. Wushu contributes to people's overall development.

51. 越来越多的外国留学生来到中国学习武术。

More and more overseas students come to China to learn Wushu.

52. 武术可以培养年轻人尊师重道、宽以待人、严于律己等高尚的道德情操。

Wushu helps young people cultivate the noble moral sentiment of respecting teachers and their teaching, being broad-minded towards others, and being strict with oneself.

53. 武术在发展过程中其内容和形式已有了很大的变化。

The content and form of Wushu have changed a lot during its process of development.

54. 功法运动是以单个运动动作为主进行练习,以达到健体或增强身体某方面机能的运动。

Gongfa focuses on single-movement practice to achieve physical fitness or strengthen certain function of the body.

55. 不同拳种不仅有不同的拳术套路,也有不同的器械套路。

Different sorts of Quan not only have different Quanshu routines, but also have different weapon routines.

56. 拳术是指徒手戏练的套路运动。

Quanshu refers to bare-handed routine movement.

57. 拳术的种类很多,常见的有长拳、南拳、太极拳、形意拳、八卦掌、翻子拳、八极拳、少林拳、象形拳等。

Quanshu includes many types of exercises, such as Changquan, Nanquan, Taichiquan, Xingyiquan, Baguazhang, Fanziquan, Bajiquan, Shaolinquan, Xiangxingquan, etc.

58. 对练是指在单练基础上,两人或两人以上,在预定条件下进行的假设性攻防练习形式。

Paired exercise refers to the forms of taolu in which two or more people exercise hypothetic attacking and defending under the prearranged conditions.

59. 搏斗运动是两人在一定条件下按照一定的规则进行斗智、较力、较技的实战攻防技术,主要包括散打、推手和短兵。

Fighting refers to practical attack and defense technique between two people under certain conditions. Fighting includes: sanda(free bare-handed fight), tuishou(push hands) and duanbing(short weapons).

60. 武术拳种纷纭、流派众多。

There are diverse sorts of Quan with various schools.

61. 据1979年全国武术收集并整理的资料显示,当时全国共有129个拳种,后来发展为131个。

National Wushu materials collected and arranged in 1979 showed that there were a total of 129 sorts of Quan throughout China and later were 131 sorts.

62. 套路可分为单练、对练和集体演练。

Routine can be divided into single person exercise, paired exercise, and group performance.

63. 对练包括徒手对练、器械对练和徒手与器械对练。

Paired exercise includes bare-handed fighting, weapon fighting and bare-handed and weapon duel.

64. 自中华人民共和国成立后,国家体育委员会把在群众中广泛流传的查、花、炮、洪、华、弹腿、少林拳等拳种,根据其共同的特点,综合整理创编了长拳。

Since the establishment of the People's Republic of China, in accordance with common characteristics, the State Sports Committee synthetically collated and created Changquan from sorts of Quan which are widespread among masses, such as Chaquan, Huaquan, Paoquan, Hongquan, Huaquan, Tantuiquan, Shaolinquan, etc.

65. 长拳是在近几十年发展起来的,以套路为主的新拳种。

Changquan has been developed in recent decades which is a new sort of Quan with routine as the main form.

66. 长拳的特点是:动作舒展大方、快速有力、节奏明显,并多起伏转折。

Characteristics of Changquan are: expansive and decent movements, speediness and power, obvious rhythm, as well as being rich in rising and turning.

67. 长拳内容包括基本功、单练套路、对练套路等。

Contents of Changquan include basic skills, single-person routine and paired routine, etc.

68. 长拳动作舒展,关节活动范围较大,对肌肉的弹性和韧带的柔韧性都有较高要求。

Movements of Changquan are expanded and stretched with a wide range of joint activities, which requires high flexibility of muscles and elasticity of ligaments.

69. 长拳的手法,要迅疾、敏捷、有力,须拳如流星。

Hand techniques of Changquan shall be rapid, prompt and powerful. The fist shoots like the falling star.

70. 长拳的眼法,要明快、锐利,须眼似电。

Eye techniques of Changquan require bright and sharp eyes. The eyes stare out like electricity.

71. 眼法在长拳运动中不是单独活动的,眼必须随手动。

Eye techniques are not individually acted in Changquan. Eyes shall follow hands.

72. 身法在长拳运动里,可分为内、转、展、缩、折、弯、俯、仰等。

In Changquan, the body movement techniques include: nei, zhuan, zhan, suo, zhe, wan, fu, yang and so on.

73. 长拳的呼吸方法,除了沉之外,还有提、托、聚、沉四法。

Other than dropping breath, Changquan's ways for breathing also include raising, holding, collecting and dropping.

74. 内三合是指心与意合,意与气合,气与力合;外三合指手与足合,肘与膝合,肩与胯合。

Three Internal Harmonies refers to the harmony of heart and mind, mind and qi, qi and force; Three External Harmonies refers to the harmony of hand and foot, elbow and knee, shoulder and hip.

75. "功"指的是力量、速度、耐力、灵敏等身体素质和运动的各种技巧。

The technique here refers to various skills in physical fitness (such as strength, speed, endurance, agility) and exercise.

76. 长拳对踢、打、摔、拿四种技击法的运动方法要求非常严格。

Changquan has very strict requirements for the methods of such four combative skills: kicking, punching, throwing, and controlling.

77. 传统的"十二形"是:动如涛、静如岳、起如猿、落如鹊、立如鸡、站如松、转如轮、折如弓、轻如叶、重如铁、缓如鹰、快如风。

Traditional 12 postures of Changquan exercise: moving like waves, being still like a mountain, rising like a monkey, falling like a magpie, erecting like a rooster, standing like a pine, turning like a wheel, bending like a bow, being light like a leaf, being heavy like iron, being slow like an eagle, and being quick like wind.

78. 长拳的精神,需要充沛、饱满。

The spirit of Changquan exercise needs to be energetic and full.

79. 体松心静是太极拳的运动特点之一。

The relaxed body and quiet heart is one of the movement characteristics of Taichi.

80. 体松是指在练拳时身体肌肉处于一种放松的状态,使身体自然舒展。

The relaxed body means that the body muscles are in a relaxing state during practice and the body is naturally stretched.

81. 心静是指练拳时要排除一切杂念,注意力要集中。

The quiet heart means that you should get rid of all distractions and focus your attention.

82. 柔的前提是要放松,在此基础上使两臂的姿势及运动路线保持弧形。

The premise of softness is to relax. On this basis, the posture of two arms and moving lines shall be maintained in a curve.

83. 初学时要保持自然呼吸,练习到一定程度时,须将呼吸、意念相配合。

The breath of the beginners shall be natural. After some practice, the coordination of breath and mind is required.

84. 道家是中国古老的哲学流派之一,它以阴阳学说为代表,表现为气的连贯流动。

Taoism is one of old philosophies of China represented by the yin and yang theory which expresses the continuous flow of qi.

85. 刀是武术短兵器的一种,为"百兵之帅",是中国最早和最普遍使用的兵器之一,它由古代兵器演变而来。

Knife known as the leader of weapons, is one of the earliest and most commonly used weapons in China which evolved from the ancient weapons.

86. 枪由上古矛戈发展演变而成,宋代以后品种繁多。

Spear is evolved from the ancient lance. There have been various sorts since the Song Dynasty.

87．枪术的主要运动特点是力贯枪尖、翻转自如、灵活多变、节奏明快、变幻莫测。

The main movement characteristics of spear are force through spear tip, upside and down easily, flexible, fast-paced, unpredictable.

88．枪的构造特点决定了其自身的运动规律。

The spear's structural feature determines its own law of motion.

89．无极的概念通常和中国的阴阳概念联系在一起。

The notion of "supreme ultimate" is often associated with the Chinese concepts of yin and yang.

90．剑术带有几分文气、优雅，又被称为"百兵之秀"。

The swordsmanship has a sort of elegance and it is also known as the God of weapons.

91．太极拳的中心思想就是使气畅通于全身。

The central idea of Taichi is that we let qi flow throughout the whole body.

92．太极拳起源于武术,通过缓慢、柔和的动作及气息的调节达到增强体质的目的。

Derived from Wushu, Taichi is composed of slow and gentle movements, mediation of breathing to strengthen people's physique.

93．太极拳大概在公元19世纪开始在中国发展起来,它源于武术或者是徒手自卫防身的练习方法。

Taichi probably developed in China in the 19th century. It is derived from Wushu, or a practice for self-defense, usually without weapons.

94．太极拳是中国武术的一个重要部分,被称为哲拳。

Taichi is an important part of Chinese martial arts and is called philosophy boxing.

95．关于太极拳的起源有不同的说法。

There are different sayings about the origin of Taichi.

96．太极拳教练经常提醒人们在刚吃完饭或很劳累或思维很活跃时不要练习太极拳。

Taichi instructors often recommend that people not practise Taichi right after their dinner, or when they are very tired, or when they have an active mind.

97. 太极拳以哲学思想为依据,提倡身、心、意的平衡。

Taichi, based on the philosophical ideas, advocates a balance of the body, mind and spirit.

98. 练成太极拳的正确姿势,以及提高柔韧性和灵活性需要很长时间,所以不要感到气馁。

It takes a long time to perform the right posture of Taichi, and improve flexibility and agility, so don't get discouraged.

99. 在美国,从健康的目的出发,太极拳早已经成为辅助治疗的一种方法。

In the United States, for the health purpose, Taichi has already been a method of adjuvant therapy.

100. 太极拳是一项负荷较小,运动量适中,能增强体质,有助于放松身体和锻炼脑部的运动。

Taichi is a kind of lower-load, moderate exercise that improves physical quality, relaxes the body and exercises the mind.

101. 有些太极拳动作的名字来自动物,比如白鹤亮翅。

Some Taichi movements are named for animals, such as White Crane Spread Its Wings.

102. 除了动作,太极拳另外两个重要的要素就是呼吸和调节。

In addition to movement, two other important elements of Taichi are breath and mediation.

103. 练习者相信太极拳的呼吸和调节有很多好处,比如,有利于内部器官的按摩和肺部气体的交换。

Practitioners believe that there are many benefits in Taichi breath and mediation, such as massaging the internal organs and the exchange of gas in the lungs.

104. 太极拳的另一个理念就是阴阳之气应该保持平衡。

Another concept of Taichi is that the forces of yin and yang should be balanced.

105. 在中国的哲学理念里,阴阳是(构成宇宙和任何事物对立统一的)两个方面。

In Chinese philosophy, yin and yang are two aspects that make up the universe and are of the unity of opposites in anything.

106. 阴被认为有水的特质,比如,寒冷、黑暗、向内和向下,有柔的特性。

Yin is believed to have the qualities of water, such as coolness, darkness, and inward and downward directions, and to be in feminine.

107. 阳被认为有火的特性,比如,热、光和向上、向外的动作,有刚的特性。

Yang is believed to have the qualities of fire, such as heat, light, and upward and outward movements, and to be in masculine.

108. 根据这种理念,人们的阴阳之气只有保持平衡才能使身体健康,而太极就是维持这种平衡的一种练习。

According to this idea, people's yin and yang need to be in balance in order to be healthy, and Taichi is a practice that maintains this balance.

109. 许多人练习太极拳的目的是为了健康,它在中国和其他许多国家被广泛练习。

Many people practise Taichi for the health purpose. Taichi is widely practised in China and in many other countries.

110. 如果你练习太极拳的姿势不正确或者你过度练习,你的肌肉可能酸痛或者扭伤。

If you don't position your body properly while practising Taichi or if you overdo practice, you may get sore muscles or sprains.

111. 阴和阳就像黑暗和光明一样,是宇宙中对立又互相联系的两个方面。

Yin and yang are opposite and interrelated in the universe like darkness and light.

112. 太极拳作为一种辅助治疗手段不能代替常规治疗或者是推迟治疗。

Taichi, as a method of adjuvant therapy, can not be used to replace conventional medical care or to delay medical care.

113. 长拳的身法要柔韧、灵活、自如,须腰如蛇行。

The body movement techniques of Changquan should be pliable, flexible and smooth. The waist shall move like a snake.

114. 很多人已经发现太极拳缓慢舒展的动作对于治疗包括头痛、高血压、关节炎、背痛、腕管综合征、消化和神经病症在内的健康问题都十分有效。

Many people have found that the slow and gentle movement of Taichi is an effective therapy for a wide range of health problems including headache, high blood pressure, arthritis, back pain, carpal tunnel syndrome, digestive and nervous disorders.

115. 那些练习太极拳的人平衡能力和柔韧性都有所提高,呼吸系统、循环系统和淋巴系统都得到加强,同时练习太极拳能降低血压,减轻疼痛并能提高生活质量。

Those who practise Taichi are rewarded with improved balance and flexibility, superior breathing, stronger circulatory and lymphatic systems, and meanwhile Taichi exercise can reduce blood tension, relieve pain, and improve living quality.

116. 缓慢、柔和的套路动作练习,使呼吸能力得到提高,从而使膈肌向外向下扩张,向内向上收缩。

The breathing ability promoted by the slow and gentle practice of routine causes the diaphragm to expand outwards and downwards and contract inwards and upwards.

117. 从肺里呼出陈腐之气,吸进新鲜之气,增大肺的容量,拉伸肌肉,减轻压力,同时给全身提供新鲜的氧气和营养素。

Exhaling stale air from the lungs while inhaling a plentitude of fresh air increases lung capacity, stretches the muscles, and releases tension. At the same time, the entire body is supplied with fresh oxygen and nutrients.

118. 太极拳的练习对人的健康非常有益。同时它还是一种精细的、复杂的、科学的防身自卫的方法。

The practice of Taichi is beneficial to people's health and it is also a subtle, sophisticated and scientific method of self-defense.

119. 太极拳适合不同年龄段的人练习,同时对场地和器材也没有什么太高的要求,在世界上已经被人们广泛接受。

Taichi is suitable for people of all ages to practise and doesn't have a high requirement for field or equipment. It has a widespread reception in the world.

120. 一套简化的太极拳,24个动作,按正常速度需要5~6分钟完成,动作缓慢但要连贯。

A set of simplified Taichi has 24 movements, which shall be finished between 5 and 6 minutes according to the normal speed. The movements should be slow but continuous.

121. 太极拳可以在室内和室外相对较小的场地上练习。当你进行缓慢、放松的练习时,太极拳通过深而规律的呼吸再加上膈肌的收缩和舒张的复杂运动,对身体的肌肉和关节进行平衡训练。

Taichi can be practised in a relatively small area either indoors or outdoors. When performed in a slow and relaxed manner, Taichi offers a balanced drill for the body's muscles and joints through deep and regulated breath and the contraction and expansion of the diaphragm.

122. 膈肌的轻柔运动按摩了肝脏和肠,而深呼吸又使得肺部的摄氧量比平时增加了许多。

This gentle movement of the diaphragm massages the liver and intestines. Deep breathing also promotes a greater intake of air into the lungs than usual.

123. 手的运动使得练习的人可以专注于动作,从而达到心神宁静的状态。

The performance of the hand creates a tranquil state of mind through concentration on the movements.

124. 胃部肌肉的练习在刺激消化、改善胃口的同时,还能预防便秘。

The exercise of stomach muscles will stimulate digestion, improve appetite and prevent constipation.

125. 优美的太极拳动作可以使我们改变不良的姿势,使心态更加平和,不容易生气。

The graceful movements of Taichi can change our inappropriate gestures, making us more even-tempered and not easy to get angry.

126. 太极这个术语指的是中国古代宇宙论中两个相反又相互作用的力(即阴和阳)的概念。

The term Taichi refers to the ancient Chinese cosmological concept of the interplay between two opposite yet interacted forces (yin and yang) as being the foundation of creation.

127. 太极拳作为武术,它的基础原理就是以柔克刚。

Taichi as martial arts, is based on the principle of softness overcoming hardness.

128. 四两拨千斤的功夫靠的不是蛮力,就像一个80多岁的人击败多人进攻不是靠他的速度一个道理。

Accomplishing a great task with little effort by clever maneuvers doesn't depend on brute strength, as a man in his eighties who is able to defend himself against multiple attackers doesn't rely upon his speed.

129. 太极拳技术包括基本功练习、桩功练习、单个动作的重复练习、组合练习、功力练习、兵器练习、技术练习和多种两人训练。

Taichi techniques include basic exercise, stance keeping exercise, repetitive single movement exercise, linked form exercise, power exercise, weapon exercise, technique exercise and various kinds of two-person exercise.

130. 训练练习可以分成两大类:单人练习和有伙伴的配合练习。

Training exercises can be divided into two broad categories: solo exercise and exercise which requires a partner.

131. 初练者通常从基本的练习开始,包括正确的框架性动作和移动身体的正确方法、重心的转换、步法等。

A beginner usually begins with the basic exercises, including proper structural alignment and correct methods of moving the body, shifting the weight, stepping position, etc.

132. 学生还将学习不同的站桩姿势,以便更利于基本动作的放松和调整以及站立冥想时的精神放松。

Students will learn different stance postures which is more beneficial to the relaxation and adjustment of the basic movements as well as a kind of mind relaxation while standing in deep thought.

133. 全身都要处于一种动态的放松,以使全身的力量都通过手毫无阻滞地到达对手身上。

The entire body is held in a state of dynamic relaxation which allows the strength of the whole body to flow into the opponent without obstruction through the hand.

134. 用蛮力或者用直力进攻对方都是严厉禁止的。

Opposing the opponent using brute strength or direct strength is strictly prohibited.

135. 练习者必须要培养粘住对手、让对方发不出力并破坏对方平衡的能力。

One must cultivate the ability to stick to the opponent, smother his strength and destroy his balance.

136. "沾、连、粘、随"的技术在太极拳实战中非常重要。

The technique (sticking, adhering, continuing and following) is quite vital to the application of Taichi combat.

137. 近年来现代太极拳在全世界越来越受欢迎,因为人们发现现代太极拳套路对调节心情、放松身体、减轻压力和整体提高健康非常有效果。

The modern routine of Taichi is becoming more and more popular worldwide in recent years because people have found it to be very conductive to calming the mind, relaxing the body, relieving stress, and improving one's health in general.

138. 杨氏太极拳的特点是动作轻柔、连绵不断。

The Yang style Taichi is characterized by soft, smooth and flowing movements.

139. 吴氏太极拳的特点是步法较高,动作紧凑,动作走弧形。

The Wu style Taichi features higher stances and compact, circular movements.

140. 形意拳和八卦掌的加入使得孙氏太极拳有了不同的韵味。

The addition of Xingyiquan and Baguazhang gives the Sun style Taichi a different flavor.

141. 太极拳的训练主要是为了放松、舒展身体。

The training of Taichi is mainly to relax and stretch the body.

142. 当你和敌人战斗时,如果你能后发先至,你就会赢。

When you fight with your enemies, if you can reach first by striking after an opponent has struck, you will win.

143. "引进落空"类似于不要以力制力的原理。

"Falling into emptiness" is analogous to the principle of never using force against force.

144. 粘连指的是你们两个人在运动时一直以柔和、不对抗的力贴着你的对手,不要分开。

Sticking and adhering refers to connecting with the opponent in a soft and non-confrontational manner and maintaining this connection as you both move.

145. 相随也就是"舍己从人",指的是要根据对手的运动和变化而不断变化以保持粘连。

Following refers to "giving up oneself and following the others" by continuously following the opponent's movement and changes in order to maintain your connection.

146. 通常,太极拳高手都是通过上肢和手臂的接触来控制对手。

Most often, Taichi advanced fighters will control the opponent through contact with his arms and upper torso.

147. 太极拳关于呼吸法的要求是:虚灵顶劲,气沉丹田。

Requirements of the breathing method of Taichi: be empty on the top of the head and qi sinks to dantian.

148. 开始学习太极拳时一般宜用自然呼吸,不宜深呼吸。

It is appropriate to breath naturally instead of holding deep breath at the beginning of learning Taichi.

149. 太极拳哲理植根于道教,是内家拳的一种。

Taichi has its philosophical root in Taoism and is considered as one kind of inner-school boxing.

150. 缓慢、柔和也是太极拳的特点。

Being slow and gentle are also the characteristics of Taichi.

151. 太极拳利用的是内气,遵循柔能克刚的原理。

Taichi utilizes the internal qi, and follows the principle: softness can overcome strength.

第二章
CHAPTER 2

武术课堂英语

WUSHU CLASSROOM ENGLISH

CHAPTER 2　WUSHU CLASSROOM ENGLISH
第二章　武术课堂英语

1. 集合！

Fall in！

2. 立正！

Attention！

3. 稍息！

Stand at ease！

4. 向右/左看齐！

Eyes right/left！

5. 向前看！

Eyes front！

6. 向中看齐！

Guide center！

7. 报数！

Count off！

8. 靠拢！

Close！

9. 散开！

Extend！

10. 齐步走！

Quick step（march）！

11. 便步走！

At ease march！

12. 跑步！

On the double！

13. 换步！

Change step！

14. 还原！

As you were！

15. 立定！

Halt！（Halt and freeze！）

16. 起立！

Get up！

17. 坐下！

Sit down!

18. 解散!

Dismiss!

19. 向后转!

About face (turn)!

20. 向右/左转!

Right/Left face (turn)!

21. 踏步,走!

Mark time, march!

22. 出列!

Out of ranks! Fall out to me!

23. 向前三步,走!

Three steps forward, march!

24. 左/右为准!

Guide left/right!

25. 以我为准!

Guide on me!

26. 前后离开一步!

Open ranks!

27. 向前靠拢!

Close ranks!

28. 点名!

Roll call!

29. 到!

Here!

30. 蹲下!

Squat down!

31. 站队!

Line up (Stand up in line)!

32. 到上课时间了。

It's time for class.

33. 现在,我们开始上课。

Now, let's begin our class.

34. 今天,我们开始教学武术基础功课程。

Today, let's start the course of Basic Skills of Wushu.

35. 现在,我们教学马步冲拳。请看完整的示范。

Now, let's learn "Punch Fist in Horse-ride Step". Please watch the complete demonstration.

36. 现在我们进行分解教学。

Now, let's start step by step.

37. 再看一次。

Watch it again.

38. 请跟我学。

Follow me, please.

39. 请听口令做练习,一、二、三、四、五、六、七、八!

Please do exercise following the command. One, two, three, four, five, six, seven, eight!

40. 重做一遍。

Once more.

41. 好!今天我们的课就上到这里,同学们,再见!

OK, time is up. Goodbye, everyone!

42. 今天,我们训练的主要内容:一是练习武术基本功;二是复习组合动作;三是整理放松。

Today, the main contents of our exercise are as follows: first, train the basic skills of Wushu; second, review the integrated movements; third, relaxing exercise.

43. 现在,我们开始训练。

Now, let's begin.

44. 首先,我们做准备活动。先做一般性准备活动,再做专项性准备活动。

Now, let's do warm-up exercise. First, we do the general warming-up; then, we do some special warm-up exercise.

45. 请大家站成两排,我们做定位操练习。

Please stand in two lines; here comes orientation exercise.

46. 请大家站成两路纵队,我们做行进间的联系。

Please stand in two rows; we are going to do marching forward.

47．下面，我们做踢腿练习。

Now let's do kicking exercise.

48．请大家一个接一个做练习。

Please do it one by one.

49．请大家跟着我做练习。

Please follow me.

50．请大家集体演练一遍。

Let's do it altogether.

51．下面，我们进行分组练习。第一组，练习"仆步抡拍"60个；第二组，练习"腾空飞脚"20个。

Next is group practice. For the first group, swing arms and pat floor in crouch step 60 times; for the second group, flying kick 20 times.

52．眼随右拳。

Eyes follow the right first.

53．外练筋骨皮，内练一口气。

Outside practises muscle skin, while inside practises one breath.

54．内外合一，神形兼备。

Pay attention to the unity of the insider and outside, spirit and form.

55．目视前方。

Eyes look ahead.

56．身体右转。

Turn the body to the right.

57．好，今天我们训练到此结束！再见！

Well, that is all for today. Bye-bye!

58．请保持你的……

please keep your...

59．头——竖直的

head—upright

60．眼睛——平视的

eyes—level

61．颈部——放松的

neck—loose

62．表情——放松的

expression—relaxed

63. 肩——要沉

shoulder—down

64. 肘——下坠

elbow—drop

65. 掌——微含的

palm—curved

66. 指——伸直的

finger—straight

67. 膝关节——微屈

knee—bent

68. 足——平的

feet—flat

69. 舌——顶上腭

tongue—roof of mouth

70. 心——静的

heart—quiet

71. 神——内敛的

thoughts—inward

72. 气——沉丹田

qi—to dantian

73. 双眼平视。

Eyes look forward.

74. 头顶保持正直。

Keep your head erect.

75. 双脚开立，与肩同宽。

Stand with your feet, shoulder-width apart.

76. 双臂自然垂于身体两侧。

Keep your arms placed naturally at your sides.

77. 上体随着膝关节的弯曲和伸直自然上下起伏。

Gently bounce your upper body up and down, bending and straightening your knee joints continuously.

78. 这个练习活动你所有的关节，做这个练习约10秒的时间。

This exercise warms up all your joints. Do this exercise for about 10 seconds.

79. 前臂自然向上抬起，轻轻晃动手臂，放松手腕。

Raise your forearms up naturally and slightly shake your arms, loosening your wrist.

80. 从左向右再从右向左转腰摆动手臂。

Swing your arms from side to side by turning your waist from the left to the right, and then from the right to the left.

81. 不要让你的膝关节运动幅度过大。

Don't allow your knee joints to move much.

82. 这个练习主要是放松你的上体。

This exercise is primarily for relaxing your upper body.

83. 左右各做10次。

Do ten times on each side.

84. 两臂向上拉伸超过头顶。

Stretch your arms over your head.

85. 双臂交叉，向右屈体同时两臂向右振动。

Circle both arms to your right while bowing to your right and begin swinging your arms down.

86. 重复5次练习然后换方向同样重复5次。

Repeat this exercise five times and then change direction for another five times.

87. 双手放于腰上顺时针和逆时针各转20次。

Place your hands on your waist and move clockwise and anticlockwise for 20 times respectively.

88. 做这个练习时，保持髋关节放松。

When doing this exercise, you should keep your hip joint relaxed.

89. 双脚并立站立。

Stand with your feet together.

90. 十指交叉，双手举过头顶。

Interlock your fingers and push both hands over your head.

91. 慢慢向左转。

Slowly turn your body to your left.

92. 身体正对前方，向右屈体。

Face front and bend your body to your right.

93. 当你做拉伸和转体时，请特别注意你的脊柱。

Please pay special attention to your spine when stretching and rotating.

94. 慢慢地放下手臂。

Slowly lower your arms down.

95. 放低手臂时保持腿部直立。

Keep your legs straight as you lower your arms.

96. 保持这种姿势数秒，接着上体左转。

Hold this position for a few seconds, and then turn your upper body to your left.

97. 慢慢站起，膝盖微屈。

Slowly stand up, and bend your knees slightly.

98. 把这个动作再重复2次。

Repeat this sequence two more times.

99. 尽可能慢地做这个拉伸动作。

Do this stretch as slowly as possible.

100. 右腿蹲下，左腿伸直。

Squat down with your right leg while keeping your left leg straight.

101. 把右手放在右膝盖上，左手放在左膝盖上。

Put your right hand on your right knee and left hand on your left knee.

102. 保持这种姿势20秒，再屈另一个腿做20秒。

Hold this position for 20 seconds, and then squat on the other leg for another 20 seconds.

103. 当做拉伸时，确保弯曲腿和脚的方向一致。

When doing this stretch, make sure that your bent leg is pointing in the same direction as your foot.

104. 以弓步姿势站立开始。

Start by standing in a bow stance.

105. 重心移至左脚。

Shift your weight to your left foot.

106. 右脚外展约45度，左脚收回靠近右脚。

Turn your right foot out about 45 degrees and bring your left foot close to your right foot.

107. 左脚前跨,脚后跟先着地。

Step forward with your left foot, touching down on your heel.

108. 向前跨步时,确保你叉步的腿不要离你的右腿太远。

When stepping forward, make sure that you don't cross your legs by stepping too far to your right leg.

109. 右脚后移,右脚掌先着地。

Step back with your right foot, touching down with the sole of your right foot first.

110. 向左跨步,重心移至左脚,接着身体左转。

Step to your left, and then turn your body to your left leg while shifting your weight to your left foot.

111. 移动右脚靠近左腿,距离约为6英寸。

Bring your right foot about 6 inches away from your left leg.

112. 身体右转,接着左脚向左跨步。

Turn your body to your right and step to your left with your left foot.

113. 向后转体,马步站立,面向前方,接着从头到尾重复此动作。

Turn your body back to face forward in a horse stance, and then repeat the exercise from the beginning to the end.

114. 重心转移至左脚时,左脚内扣,右脚外撇。

Turn your left foot in and right foot out as you shift your weight back to your left foot.

115. 右脚前跨一步,脚后跟先着地。

Step forward with your right foot, touching down with the heel of your right foot first.

116. 重心前移成弓步。

Shift your weight forward into a bow stance.

117. 手指向内微屈,手掌保持自然姿势。

The natural position of your palm is with your fingers slightly bent in.

118. 张开手掌,手指弯曲,握在一起,大拇指放在中指的第二指关节上。

Open your palm, fold your fingers in one section at a time and place your thumb on the second finger joint.

119. 保持手腕与指关节和前臂相平。

Keep your wrist even with your knuckle and forearm.

120. 握拳时,应该握紧但不要僵硬。

When holding a fist, you should grip firmly, not grip tightly.

121. 假设你的手中握的是一支易折断的铅笔芯,不要突发力。

Imagine that you have a fragile piece of pencil lead in your hand, and don't give sudden force.

122. 如果你握得太紧,铅笔芯就会折断。

If you hold your fist too tight, you will break the pencil lead.

123. 如果你握得太松,铅笔芯就会从你的手中落下。

If you hold it too loose, the pencil lead will fall out of your hand.

124. 掌心向下,指根微含。

From an open palm facing down, squeeze the base of your thumb in slightly.

125. 接着五指弯曲,捏在一起指向下方。

Then bent your five fingers, pinch together, and point to the bottom.

126. 通过运动手指,你能达到活动关节的作用。

By moving your fingers individually, you exercise the joints in your hand.

127. 起势和收势往往在同一个地方。

The commencing form and closing form are usually in the same place.

128. 大部分重心移至右脚。

Shift most of your weight to your right foot.

129. 以右脚脚掌和左脚脚后跟为轴向后转体。

Turn to your back, by pivoting on the sole of your right foot and the heel of your left foot.

130. 右脚前跨一小步,接着左脚跟上一小步,左脚掌着地。

Take a small step forward with your right foot. Then the left foot follows up with a small step, touching down with the sole of your left foot.

131. 同时,左手前推,右手收至于腰旁。

At the same time, thrust your left hand forward and bring your right hand next to your waist.

132. 左脚回收至左后方,重心移到左脚,同时提右脚,脚后跟落地。

与此同时,收回左掌,右掌前挑。

Step back to your back left corner with your left foot and shift your weight to it as you lift your right foot up and touch down with your heel. At the same time, pull your left palm back and extend your right palm forward.

133. 练习太极拳之前,让我们做些简单的拉伸练习和热身运动。

Before we practise Taichi, let us do some simple stretch and warm-up exercise.

134. 热身运动不仅可以活动身体,而且可以使大脑做好运动的准备。

Warm-up exercise is not only to get your physical body ready, but also to get your mind ready to exercise.

135. 下面一系列的热身练习可以从身体上和心理上使你更好地进行太极拳训练。

The following series of warm-up exercise will prepare you physically and mentally for your Taichi training.

136. 不能让你的上体前倾或者后仰,同时胸部要自然放松。

Don't allow your upper body to lean forward or backward. At the same time, your chest should be naturally relaxed.

137. 确保你向前跨步时,双脚不在一条直线上。

Make sure that when you step forward, your feet are not in a straight line.

138. 右脚向前半步。

Bring your right foot a half step forward.

139. 身体微微左转,同时右手向前,双掌同时翻转,掌心相对(右掌向上,左掌向下)。

Turn your body slightly to your left while extending your right hand forward and rotating both palms until they face each other—the right palm faces up and the left palm faces down.

140. 身体右转,右手抽至腰旁,左手弧形上摆直至掌心对着右方。

Turn your body to your right while lowering your right hand down to your waist and circling your left hand up with your palm facing to your right.

141. 身体继续右转,眼睛看右掌。

Turn your body further to your right, and look at your right palm.

CHAPTER 2 WUSHU CLASSROOM ENGLISH
第二章　武术课堂英语

142. 左脚轻抬,向前迈步,同时左掌经左膝搂过,右掌前推。

Lift your left foot up slightly and step forward, while beginning to brush your left palm across your left knee and extend your right palm.

143. 重心移至左脚成弓步。

Shift your weight to your left foot into a bow stance.

144. 右掌轻触左手腕,重心移至左脚,双掌同时前移。

Your right palm slightly touches your left wrist, and both palms extend forward, while shifting your weight to your left foot.

145. 身体前方提起左脚,同时抬右掌于体前。

Lift your left foot up in front of you. At the same time, lift your right palm up in front of your body.

146. 当你做这个动作时,假想你正在掷一个球。

As you do this movement, imagine that you are throwing a ball.

147. 这个动作防止你膝盖扭转受伤。

This movement will prevent your knee from being torqued.

148. 脚后跟不要离开地面,尽可能下蹲。做这个拉伸动作时可以脚尖向上。

Squat down as low as you can, without your heels leaving the floor. You can do this stretch with your toes pointing up.

149. 尽可能想象并感受你的身体充满来自宇宙和太阳的能量。

Try to imagine and feel that your body is filled with energy from the universe and the sun.

150. 每一次完成一个循环,要尽量放松你的关节、肌肉和身体的其他器官,包括头部、肩部、脖子、颈椎、肘部、髋部以及身体的内部器官。

Each time you complete a cycle, try to loosen up your joints, muscles and other organs in your body(including your head, shoulders, neck, spine, elbows, hips, and internal organs).

151. 拳自腰间旋转向前打出。

Turn your fist on the side of your waist and then thrust forwards.

152. 由拳心向上转为拳眼向上。

Turn your fist from the fist center up to the fist eye up.

153. 高不过肩,低不过胸。

Neither higher than your shoulders nor lower than your chests.

154．力达拳面。

Convey your strength to the surface of your fist.

155．搬拳。

Parry fist.

156．屈臂俯拳。

Bend your arm and make your fist downward.

157．自异侧而上。

Move from down to up on the other side.

158．以肘关节为轴,前臂翻至体前或体侧。

Make your elbow joint an axis and turn your forearm to the front side or the side of your body.

159．手臂呈弧形,腕与肩平。

Your arm is like an arc and your wrist is as high as your shoulders.

160．五指弯曲,拇指压于食指、中指第二指关节上,不可太紧或太松,拳面要平。

Curve five fingers. Put the thumb on the second knuckle of your index and middle fingers, neither too tight nor too loose. The surface of your fist should be flat.

161．五指自然舒展,掌心微含。

Stretch your five fingers naturally. The center of your palm is hollow.

162．五指第一指关节自然捏拢,屈腕使勾尖自然朝下,不可过于用力下勾。

Close the first knuckle of your five fingers together naturally. Bend your wrist so that the hook tip faces downwards naturally. Don't over bend your wrist.

163．双臂向下经两侧,臂内旋,向前上方弧形圈打,腕与耳同高。

Your fists sweep from the downward sides of your body. Turn arms inwards, sweep and punch forwards and upwards in a curve. Your wrists are as high as your ears.

164．单推掌

single palm pushing

165．臂由屈到伸,掌经耳旁、肩上,后臂内旋,立掌向前推出,腕与肩平,力达掌根。

Bend your arm and then stretch your arm. Push forward from your ear and upper shoulder. Your arm turns inwards. Stand your palm and push forwards. Your wrist should be as high as your shoulder. Convey your strength to the palm root.

166．单按推掌

single press and palm pushing

167．臂由屈到伸,掌自腰间立,掌向前按推。

Bend your arm and then stretch it. Stand your palm, press and push forwards from your waist.

168．双推掌

double palm pushing

169．臂由屈到伸,两掌自然立于胸前,同时向前按推,高不过肩,低不过胸,立达掌根。

Bend your arm and then stretch your arm. Stand your palms before your chests. Press and push simultaneously, neither higher than your shoulders nor lower than your chests. Convey your strength to the palm root.

170．搂掌

brush palm

171．掌自异侧经体前呈弧形下搂至膝外侧,落至胯旁。

Move your palm from the other side of your body, pass through the front side of your body to the outer side of your knee in a shape of an arc, and stop your palm beside your hip.

172．基本原则

basic principle

173．身体和精神完全放松

body & mind completely relaxed

174．呼吸和动作协调一致

breath & movement coordinate

175．运动舒展,不要紧张。

Move comfortably, and don't strain.

176．整体要开不要缩。

Open, and don't stretch.

177．注意力100%集中于动作。

Attention on movements.

178. 当练习太极拳的时候，思想必须要安静下来，呼吸要缓慢、细长，和动作结合起来。

When practising Taichi, you must calm down your thoughts, and breathe deeply and slowly, combining with your movements.

179. 头部保持正直，表情放松，眼睛外看但又不要特别专注于某物。

Your head is erect, expression relaxed, eyes looking out but not focused on anything in particular.

180. 同学们，今天让我们来学习太极拳的基本动作。

Guys, let's learn Taichi basic movements today.

181. 请听我的口令，前排侧平举，后排前平举，成体操队行散开。

Arms out and stand in lines as my follow, please.

182. 在进行太极拳的套路之前，让我们做一下热身运动和呼吸练习。

Let's do some warm-up and breathing exercise before we start doing routine.

183. 请注意你的身体姿势。

Please pay attention to your body posture.

184. 太极拳对上肢部分的要求是沉肩、垂肘、坐腕、突掌并旋腕转膀。

Demands of Taichi for the upper limb are: drop your shoulders and elbows, wrists, and stick out your palms and twist your shoulders.

185. 集体复习三遍、分组练习三遍、教学比赛一遍。

Three times for collective review, three times in groups, and teaching competition once.

186. 下面的教学与训练内容，供教师和学习者参考。

The following teaching and training arrangements are for teachers' and learners' reference.

187. 分段教学动作路线、方向、要点可采用分解、慢练的形式引导学员练习动作，掌握技术。

Section teaching, including the route of movement, direction, points can adopt step-by-step teaching and slow practising to help learners learn and master techniques.

188. 初级棍术的演练要求是：动作快速勇猛，棍法干净利落，有"棍打一大片"的说法。

Primary cugdelplay requires practitioners to be quick and valorous, with the positions neat and determined, as a saying goes, "A stick sweeps a crowd."

189. 初级刀术的演练要求是：动作勇猛快速，刀法呼呼生风，气势咄咄逼人，有"刀如猛虎"之说。

Primary broadswordplay requires the practitioners to move swiftly, with the broadsword whirling in aggressive vigor, as a saying goes, "The knife is like a fierce tiger."

190. 完整示范法帮助学生建立一个整体的印象，使其对将要学习的动作有一个完整的认识。

A method of complete demonstration helps students establish a general impression and get a complete recognition of the whole set.

191. 先学掌、拳、勾3种手形和手法，以及弓步、马步、仆步、虚步、歇步5种步形和步法的单个动作，然后再练习两个或两个以上的组合动作，并逐渐过渡到整套组合动作的练习。

First learn three hand forms and positions: palm, fist and hook forms, and five foot forms and positions: bow step, horse-ride step, crouch step, empty step and seated step. After mastering every single movement, learners can exercise a simple set of two movements or more, and gradually transmit to a set of combined movements.

192. 待动作熟练后，可左右势互换，进行重复练习。

After having skillfully practised the movements, learners can practise alternately on the left side and the right side repeatedly.

193. 分解是把动作难点、要点和动作路线、方向、力点交代清楚，使学生对所学动作有一个较深的认识。

Step-by-step teaching deals with difficult parts and key points, the route, directions and point of force in detail, and therefore, learners can get a rather deep understanding of the movements they are learning.

194. 一般方法是：先示范，再分解教学，最后领做。

To be general, first demonstrate, then teach step by step, and at last lead learners to exercise.

195. 你要尽量放松,释放身体和精神的所有压力。

You should try to relax, and release all tension within your body and mind.

196. 所有的关节稍微弯曲。

Bend all joints slightly.

197. 不要着急,尽量体会、享受、沉浸进去。

Don't hurry. Try to enjoy, feel and sink.

198. 拳眼斜朝下,两臂呈弧形。

Fist-eyes are obliquely downward, and bend arms like arcs.

199. 虎口呈弧形,手指既不可僵直也不可放松弯曲。

A part between the thumb and the index finger is like an arc. Your fingers are neither too stiff nor too loose and bent.

200. 左脚后撤一步成弓步,掌心向下。

Withdraw your left foot back a step into a bow step and the palm is down.

201. 劈掌时力达掌沿,冲拳时要与拧腰配合。

Cutting force should reach the palm edge. Punching the fist and twisting the waist should be done coordinately.

第三章
CHAPTER 3
武术套路英语教学
WUSHU ROUTINE ENGLISH TEACHING

一、五步拳
Section Ⅰ Five-step Boxing

五步拳是结合长拳的步型、步法、手型、手法编排而成的基础套路练习。动作简单,易学易练。整套演练的要求是:动作规范,舒展大方,刚劲有力。其套路主要由弓步、马步、仆步、虚步、歇步5种步型结合搂手、冲拳、按掌、穿掌、挑掌、架打等手型、手法编排而成。全套共有8个动作。

Five-step boxing is basic routine exercise combined with step forms, step positions, hand forms and hand positions of long boxing. It is simple and easy to learn and exercise. The general requirement is standardized, comfortable and powerful in movements. It is mainly a combination of five step forms (bow step, horse-ride step, crouch step, empty step and seated step), hand forms and hand positions (brush hand, thrust fist, press palm, penetrate palm, block palm, uphold and punch and etc.). The whole set includes 8 movements.

(一)五步拳动作名称

Movement Names of Five-step Boxing

1. 起势:并步抱拳

Commencing Form:Join Feet with Fists at the Waist

(1)弓步冲拳

Punch Fist in Bow Step

(2)弹腿冲拳

Spring Leg and Punch Fist

(3)马步架打

Strike Out One Fist with the Other Upheld in Horse-ride Step

(4)歇步盖打

Thump Down and Punch Fist in Seated Step

(5)提膝穿掌

Lift Knee and Penetrate Palm

（6）仆步插掌

Thrust Palm in Crouch Step

（7）虚步挑拳

Stick Up Palm in Empty Step

（8）并步抱拳

Join Feet with Fists at the Waist

2. 收势

Closing Form

（二）五步拳动作过程

Movement Processes of Five-step Boxing

1. 起势：并步抱拳

Commencing Form：Join Feet with Fists at the Waist

　　　　　　　　　　　a　　　　　　b

图 1-1　　　　　　　　　　图 1-2

（1）弓步冲拳（图 1-3）

Punch Fist in Bow Step(Picture 1-3)

　　左脚向左前迈步成左弓步，同时左手向左平搂，收回腰间抱拳，右拳向前冲出，目视前方。

Step the left foot forward with the knee bent in a bow step. Meanwhile make a level sweeping movement with the left hand, return the hand to the waist into a fist, and then punch forward the right fist, eyes looking straight ahead.

CHAPTER 3　WUSHU ROUTINE ENGLISH TEACHING
第三章　武术套路英语教学

图 1-3

（2）弹腿冲拳（图 1-4）
Spring Leg and Punch Fist（Picture 1-4）

图 1-4

重心前移,右腿向前弹踢,同时冲左拳,收右拳,目视前方。

Move your center of gravity forward. Kick forward the right leg and meanwhile punch the left fist and draw the right fist back, eyes looking straight ahead.

（3）马步架打（图1-5）

Strike Out One Fist with the Other Upheld in Horse-ride Step (Picture 1-5)

a（正面）

b（背面）

图 1-5

上身左转 90°,下蹲成马步,同时左拳变掌,屈左臂上架,冲右拳,目视右拳。

Turn the upper body 90° to the left, knees bent, legs apart in a horse-ride step. Meanwhile change the left fist into a palm and raise the left arm over the head. Punch the right fist, eyes following the right fist.

（4）歇步盖打（图1-6）

Thump Down and Punch Fist in Seated Step (Picture 1-6)

左脚向右脚后插一步,上身左转 90°,同时右拳变掌向左下盖,收左拳抱于腰间,目视右掌；两腿屈膝下蹲成歇步,冲左拳,收右拳至腰间,目视左拳。

Step the left foot behind the right one while turning the upper body 90° to the left. Meanwhile change the right fist into a palm and thump down to the left side. Draw back the left fist to the waist, eyes following the right palm. Bend the knees in a seated step, punch the left fist, and draw back the right fist to the waist, eyes following the left fist.

CHAPTER 3　WUSHU ROUTINE ENGLISH TEACHING
第三章　武术套路英语教学

a　　　　　　　　　　b

c　　　　　　　　　　d

图 1-6

（5）提膝穿掌（图 1-7）

Lift Knee and Penetrate Palm(Picture 1-7)

a(正面)　　　　　　　　b(背面)

图 1-7

身体右转。随即左拳变掌,顺势收至右腋下。右拳变掌,从左手背上穿出,手心向上,同时左腿屈膝提起,目视右掌。

Turn the body to the right. Change the left fist into a palm, and move it to the right armpit. Change the right fist into a palm and penetrate it upward from the back of the left hand, palm facing up. Meanwhile bend the left knee and raise the left leg, eyes following the right palm.

(6) 仆步插掌(图1-8)

Thrust Palm in Crouch Step(Picture 1-8)

图 1-8

屈右膝,左脚落地成仆步;左掌手指朝前,沿左腿内侧穿至左脚面,目视左掌。

Bend the right knee and extend the left foot in a crouch step. Stab fingers of the left palm forward from inside of the left leg to the left instep, eyes following the left palm.

(7) 虚步挑掌(图1-9)

Stick Up Palm in Empty Step (Picture 1-9)

图 1-9

左腿屈膝前弓,右脚上前成虚步,同时左手向左划弧成勾手,顺右腿外侧向上挑右掌,目视右方。

Bend the left leg, and step the right foot forward into an empty step. Meanwhile draw an arc with the left hand in the hook form, and stick up the right palm from outside of the right leg, eyes looking the right.

(8) 并步抱拳(图 1-2-b)

Join Feet with Fists at the Waist(Picture 1-2-b)

左脚向右脚靠拢成并步。同时双手变拳,收拳至腰间,目视左方。

Join the left foot to the right foot. Meanwhile change both hands into fists and draw them back to the waist, eyes looking the left.

2. 收势(图 1-2-a)

Closing Form(Picture 1-2-a)

两臂放下,位于体侧,目视前方。

Hang both arms down aside and look ahead.

二、八式太极拳

Section Ⅱ　8-form Taichi

(一) 八式太极拳动作名称

Movement Names of 8-form Taichi

1. 起势

Commencing Form

(1) 倒卷肱

Step Back and Whirl on Both Sides

(2) 搂膝拗步

Brush Knee and Twist Step

(3) 野马分鬃

Part Wild Horse's Mane

(4) 云手

Wave Hands like Clouds

(5) 金鸡独立

Golden Rooster Stands on One Leg

（6）蹬脚

Kick with Heel

（7）拦雀尾

Grasp Sparrow's Tail

（8）十字手

Cross Hands

2. 收势

Closing Form

（二）八式太极拳动作过程

Movement Processes of 8-form Taichi

1. 起势（图 2-1）

Commencing Form（Picture 2-1）

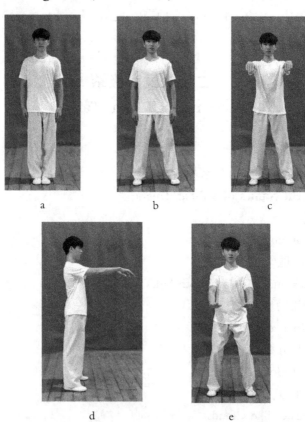

图 2-1

① 双脚并拢,两臂轻贴身体两侧。(自然呼吸数次)

Stand with your feet together and your arms stick to your sides. (inhale and exhale naturally a few times)

② 双膝微屈,左脚向左轻分开,与肩同宽。

Bend your knees slightly, and then step to your left with your left foot, shoulder width apart.

③ 双掌抬至肩平,掌心向下。

Raise your arms up to the shoulder level, palms facing down.

④ 微微屈双膝,两臂落到腹部水平。(呼气)

While bending your knees slightly, lower your arms to the abdomen level. (exhale)

(1) 倒卷肱(图2-2)

Step Back and Whirl on Both Sides (Picture 2-2)

a　　　　　　　　　　b

图2-2

① 左肘稍弯曲,转腰向右,同时收右掌至腰间,左掌向前。

Bend your left elbow slightly and pivot your waist to the right. Meanwhile draw back your right palm to your waist and extend your left palm forward.

② 右臂前伸向上,翻转双掌,掌心向上。(吸气)

Extend your right arm out and up, and rotate both palms facing up. (inhale)

③ 右肘弯曲,转腰向左,同时收左掌至腰间,右掌前伸。(呼气)

Bend your right elbow and pivot your waist to the left. Meanwhile draw back the left palm to your waist and extend the right palm forward. (exhale)

④ 左臂前伸向上,翻转双掌,掌心向上。(吸气)

Extend your left arm out and up, and rotate both palms facing up. (inhale)

⑤ 左肘弯曲,转腰向右,同时收右掌至腰间,左掌向前。(呼气)

Bend your left elbow and pivot your waist to your right. Meanwhile draw back your right palm to your waist and extend your left palm forward. (exhale)

(2) 搂膝拗步(图2-3)

Brush Knee and Twist Step (Picture 2-3)

a

b

图2-3

① 身体稍向右转,右手放低,双眼注视右掌。

Turn your body slightly to your right and lower your right hand. Eyes look at your right palm.

② 左脚轻抬,身体左转,同时左脚向前踏出。左掌划过左膝,右掌前推。(呼气)

Lift your left foot up slightly and turn your body to your left while stepping forward with your left foot. Your left palm brushes your left knee and you extend your right palm forward. (exhale)

③ 重心移至左脚成弓步,右掌前推。

Shift your center of gravity to your left foot into a bow step and extend your right palm forward.

④ 身体后坐,重心移至右脚,左脚内转,同时右掌内翻,收左掌至腹部。(吸气)

Sit back and shift your center of gravity to your right foot. Turn your left foot in while rotating your right palm in and drawing back your left palm to your abdomen. (inhale)

⑤ 右脚向左脚并拢,同时左臂向上划弧与头齐平,右掌下压,掌心向下。

Bring your right foot close to your left foot and meanwhile circle your left arm up to the head level. Lower your right palm to face down.

⑥ 重心移至右脚成弓步,左掌前推。

Shift your center of gravity to your right foot into a bow step and extend your left palm forward.

⑦ 右脚向前踏出,同时右掌划过右膝,左掌前推。(吸气)

Step forward with your right foot. Meanwhile your right palm brushes your right knee and you extend your left palm forward. (inhale)

(3) 野马分鬃(图2-4)

Part Wild Horse's Mane (Picture 2-4)

　　　a　　　　　　b　　　　　　c　　　　　　d

图 2-4

① 重心后移至左脚。(吸气)

Shift your center of gravity back to your left foot. (inhale)

② 右脚内转,重心移至右脚,同时身体左转,翻右掌直至掌面向下,左手随身体转动而向前划弧。

Turn your right foot in and shift your center of gravity to it, while turning your body to the left. Rotate your right palm until it faces down, and let your left hand circle forward with the rotation of your body.

③ 左脚移至右脚侧,同时收右掌至胸前,掌心向下。收左掌至腹部,掌心向上。

Bring your left foot next to your right foot while drawing back your right palm to your chest, palm facing down. Draw back your left palm to your abdomen, palm facing up.

④ 左脚前踏,脚跟先触地。身体左转,同时向下收右掌,左掌前推。(呼气)

Step forward with your left foot, touching down with your heel first. Turn your body to the left while pulling your right palm down and extending your left palm forward. (exhale)

⑤ 重心移至左侧成弓步,同时左掌前推,直至与眼齐平,右掌下压至胯旁。

Shift your center of gravity to the left in a bow step while extending your left palm forward, until it is on the eye level, and lower your right palm until it is next to your hip.

⑥ 身体后坐,重心移至右脚,同时移左掌至胸侧,掌心向下。收右掌至腹部,掌心向上,好似抱球。

Sit back and shift your center of gravity back to your right foot while bringing your left palm next to your chest, palm facing down. Draw back your right palm to your abdomen, palm facing up, just like holding a ball.

⑦ 右脚移至左脚侧,紧接着右脚前踏,脚跟先着地。重心移至右侧成弓步,同时右掌前推,直至与眼齐平,左掌下压至胯旁。

Bring your right foot next to your left foot and step forward with your right foot, touching down with your heel first. Shift your center of gravity to the right in a bow step while extending your right palm forward, until it is on the eye level, and lower your left palm until it is next to your hip.

(4) 云手(图2-5)

Wave Hands like Clouds (Picture 2-5)

图 2-5

① 身体后坐,右脚内转,同时双臂划弧至身体左侧。

Sit back and turn your right foot in while circling your arms to your left.

② 向左踏步,继续前面图 2-5-a 的动作。

Step to the left and continue the previous movement of Picture 2-5-a.

③ 左掌掌心向上,继续划弧过面部,同时右手下压,收右脚至左脚侧。(呼气)

Your left palm faces up, and continue circling across your face while lowering your right hand and drawing back your right foot close to your left foot. (exhale)

④ 继续前面图 2-5-c 的动作,收左掌,抬右掌。

Continue the previous movement of Picture 2-5-c, lowering your left palm and lifting your right palm.

⑤ 向左踏步,同时右掌前推至体侧,掌心向下,此时左掌掌心向上开始上提。(吸气)

Step to your left while extending your right palm to the side of your body, palm facing down, and begin lifting your left palm up. (inhale)

⑥ 重心从左脚移至右脚,保持双臂划弧。

Shift your center of gravity from your left foot to your right foot and keep circling your arms.

⑦ 重心移至左脚,同时右手划弧向下,左手掌心向上划过头部。(吸气)

Shift your center of gravity to the left foot while the right hand circles down, and the left palm crosses the head. (inhale)

(5) 金鸡独立(图2-6)

Golden Rooster Stands on One Leg (Picture 2-6)

a b c d

图 2-6

① 重心移至左脚,同时向下收双掌。(吸气)

Shift your center of gravity to your left foot while lowering your right and left palms. (inhale)

② 左脚外转,重心前移,向下收左掌,同时立右掌。

Turn your left foot out and shift your center of gravity forward while lowering your left palm. At the same time, open your right hand and spear up.

③ 右脚触地,吸气时保持脚和膝盖协调。

Touch the ground with your right foot. Keep your foot and knee in harmony while inhaling.

④ 右脚外转,重心前移,向下收右掌,同时立左掌。

Turn your right foot out and shift your center of gravity forward while lowering your right palm. At the same time, open your left hand and spear up.

CHAPTER 3 WUSHU ROUTINE ENGLISH TEACHING

（6）蹬脚（图 2-7）

Kick with Heel (Picture 2-7)

a

b

图 2-7

① 左脚移至右脚侧，同时双掌上下划弧，直至双臂交叉，双掌掌心向内——右掌在外侧。

Bring your left foot next to your right foot while circling both palms up and down until your arms are crossed with both palms facing inward—your right palm should be on the outside.

② 抬右脚，翻转双掌至掌心向前，紧接着分双掌至身体两侧。（呼气）

Lift your right foot up, rotate both palms until they face forward, and begin to separate your palms to both sides of your body. (exhale)

③ 向右侧伸右腿，同时右掌向同侧推出。

Extend your right leg up to the right, while extending your right palm in the same direction.

④ 向左侧伸左腿，同时左掌向同侧推出。

Extend your left leg up to the left, while extending your left palm in the same direction.

⑤ 抬左脚，翻转双掌至掌心向前，紧接着分双掌至身体两侧。

Lift your left foot up, rotate both palms until they face forward, and begin to separate your palms to both sides of your body.

⑥ 右脚移至左脚侧，同时双掌上下划弧，直至双臂交叉，双掌掌心向内——左掌在外侧。

Bring your right foot next to the left foot while circling both palms up and down until your arms are crossed while both palms facing inward—your left palm should be on the outside.

（7）揽雀尾（图2-8）

Grasp Sparrow's Tail (Picture 2-8)

图2-8

① 双掌前推，重心移至右脚。(呼气)

Push your two palms forward and shift your center of gravity to the right foot. (exhale)

② 身体右转，向前踏步，重心前移成右弓步，同时右前臂前伸，向下收左掌。(呼气)

Turn your body to the right and step forward, shifting your center of gravity forward into a right bow stance, while extending your right forearm forward and pulling your left palm down. (exhale)

③ 双臂逆时针翻转，重心移回左脚。(吸气)

Rotate both arms counterclockwise, and then shift your center of gravity back to your left foot. (inhale)

④ 向下收双掌。(呼气)

Lower both palms. (exhale)

⑤ 双臂继续划弧并向前伸出，右拳触左掌，然后双掌前伸，同时重心移至右脚。

Continue the circular movements of your arms and begin extending them forward. Your right fist touches your left palm. Extend both palms forward, while shifting your center of gravity to your right foot.

⑥ 翻转双掌至掌心向下，在重心移至身体左侧时双掌分开。(吸气)

Rotate both palms until they face down, and separate them while shifting your center of gravity to your left. (inhale)

⑦ 双掌下压，收至腹部。

Lower both palms and draw them back to the abdomen.

⑧ 重心转至右脚时双掌向前推出。(呼气)

Push forward both palms while shifting your center of gravity to your right foot. (exhale)

⑨ 身体后坐，左脚移至右脚侧，同时双掌好似抱球(双掌掌心彼此相对)。

Sit back and bring your left foot next to your right foot while palms are just like holding a ball (palms center facing to each other).

⑩ 重复动作 b 到 i。

Repeat movements b to i.

(8) 十字手(图2-9)
Cross Hands (Picture 2-9)

a　　　　　　　　　b　　　　　　　　c

图 2-9

① 重心移至右脚,抬左脚掌,身体右转 180°。(吸气)

Shift your center of gravity to your right foot, lift the sole of your left foot up and turn your body 180° to your right. (inhale)

② 左脚内转至脚尖向前,右脚外转,同时转体,右掌向右侧推出,收左掌至身体稍左侧。

Turn your left foot in until it points forward. Turn your right foot out while you rotate your body, and extend your right palm to your right side. Pull your left palm slightly to your left side.

③ 重心移至左脚,双掌下压。(呼气)

Shift your center of gravity to your left foot and lower your palms. (exhale)

④ 右脚向左,直至双脚与肩同宽,同时抱双掌由下至上,跨过腰部至面前,右掌在外,慢慢站起,保持双膝微屈。

Bring your right foot close to your left until both feet are shoulder width apart while scooping both palms down and up. Cross your wrists to your face with your right palm on the outside. Stand up slowly, and keep your knees slightly bent.

2. 收势(图2-10)
Closing Form (Picture 2-10)

a b c

图 2-10

① 翻转双掌至掌心向下。（吸气）

Rotate both palms until they face down. (inhale)

② 分双掌，直至与肩同宽。

Separate both palms until they are shoulder width apart.

③ 双掌下压至胯部，完全站立。（呼气）

Lower both palms to the hip and stand up completely. (exhale)

④ 左脚移至右脚旁，双手垂于身体两侧。

Bring your left foot to your right foot and allow both hands to relax at both sides of your body.

第四章
CHAPTER 4

武术套路名称

NAMES OF WUSHU ROUTINE

CHAPTER 4　NAMES OF WUSHU ROUTINE
第四章　武术套路名称

一、五步拳动作名称
Section I　Movement Names of Five-step Boxing

（一）起势	**Commencing Form**
1. 弓步冲拳	Brush Hand and Punch Fist in Bow Step
2. 弹腿冲拳	Spring Leg and Punch Fist
3. 马步架打	Strike Out One Fist with the Other Upheld in Horse-ride Step
4. 歇步盖打	Thump Down and Punch Fist in Seated Step
5. 提膝穿掌	Lift Knee and Penetrate Palm
6. 仆步插掌	Thrust Palm in Crouch Step
7. 虚步挑掌	Stick Up Palm in Empty Step
8. 并步抱拳	Join Feet with Fists at the Waist
（二）收势	**Closing Form**

二、初级长拳第三路动作名称
Section II　Movement Names of Primary Long Boxing, Routine 3

（一）起势	**Commencing Form**
1. 虚步亮拳	Flash Palm in Empty Step
2. 并步对拳	Join Feet Fist to Fist
（二）第一段	**Section 1**
1. 弓步冲拳	Punch Fist in Bow Step
2. 弹腿冲拳	Spring Leg and Punch Fist
3. 大跃步前穿	Jump Forward with Long Steps and Penetrate
4. 弓步击掌	Clap Palm in Bow Step
5. 马步架掌	Strike Out Palm in Horse-ride Step
（三）第二段	**Section 2**
1. 虚步栽拳	Punch Down in Empty Step

2. 提膝穿掌　　　　　　Lift Knee and Penetrate Palm
3. 仆步穿掌　　　　　　Penetrate Palm in Crouch Step
4. 虚步挑掌　　　　　　Strike Up Palm in Empty Step
5. 马步击掌　　　　　　Clap Palm in Horse-ride Step
6. 叉步双摆掌　　　　　Swing Two Palms in Crossed Step
7. 弓步击掌　　　　　　Clap Palm in Bow Step
8. 转身踢腿,马步盘肘　　Kick Up with Body Turn and Wind Elbow in Horse-ride Step

（四）第三段　　　　　**Section 3**
1. 歇步抡砸拳　　　　　Swing Fists and Pound Down in Seated Step
2. 仆步亮掌　　　　　　Flash Palm in Crouch Step
3. 弓步劈拳　　　　　　Cut Fist in Bow Step
4. 换跳步,弓步冲拳　　　Shift Jump Feet, Punch Fist in Bow Step
5. 马步冲拳　　　　　　Punch Fist in Horse-ride Step
6. 弓步下冲拳　　　　　Punch Fist Downward in Bow Step
7. 叉步亮掌侧踹腿　　　Flash Palm in Crossed Step and Thrust Leg Sideways
8. 虚步挑拳　　　　　　Strike Up Palm in Empty Step

（五）第四段　　　　　**Section 4**
1. 弓步顶肘　　　　　　Poke with Elbow in Bow Step
2. 转身左拍脚　　　　　Turn Around and Clap Left Foot
3. 右拍脚　　　　　　　Clap Right Foot
4. 腾空飞脚　　　　　　Jump Up to Fly Foot
5. 歇步下冲拳　　　　　Punch Fist Downward in Seated Step
6. 仆步抡劈拳　　　　　Swing Fist and Pound Down in Crouch Step
7. 提膝挑掌　　　　　　Lift Knee and Strike Up Palm
8. 提膝劈掌,弓步冲拳　　Lift Knee, Cut Palm and Punch Fist in Bow Step

（六）收势　　　　　　**Closing Form**
1. 虚步亮拳　　　　　　Flash Palm in Empty Step
2. 并步对拳　　　　　　Join Feet Fist to Fist

三、初级刀术动作名称
Section III Movement Names of Primary Broadswordplay

（一）起势		Commencing Form
1. 虚步抱刀		Hold Broadsword in Empty Step
2. 并步交刀		Join Feet and Exchange Broadsword
（二）第一段		Section 1
1. 弓步缠头		Wrap Head in Bow Step
2. 虚步藏刀		Hide Broadsword in Empty Step
3. 弓步前刺		Thrust Broadsword Forward in Bow Step
4. 并步上挑		Join Feet and Block Broadsword Upward
5. 左抡劈刀		Slash with Sabre Down Leftward in Vertical Circle
6. 右抡劈刀		Slash with Sabre Down Rightward in Vertical Circle
7. 弓步撩刀		Swing Up Broadsword in Bow Step
8. 弓步藏刀		Hide Broadsword in Bow Step
（三）第二段		Section 2
1. 提膝缠头		Lift Knee and Wrap Head
2. 弓步平斩		Cut Horizontally in Bow Step
3. 仆步带刀		Bring Broadsword in Crouch Step
4. 歇步下砍		Cut Downward in Seated Step
5. 左劈刀		Cut Broadsword on the Left
6. 右劈刀		Cut Broadsword on the Right
7. 歇步按刀		Press Broadsword in Seated Step
8. 马步平劈		Cut Horizontally in Horse-ride Step
（四）第三段		Section 3
1. 弓步撩刀		Circle Broadsword in Bow Step
2. 插步反撩		Counter-circle Broadsword in Inserting Step
3. 转身挂劈		Turn Around, Row and Cut
4. 仆步下砍		Cut Downward in Crouch Step
5. 架刀前刺		Raise Broadsword and Thrust Forward

	6. 左斜劈	Cut Broadsword on the Left Diagonal
	7. 右斜劈	Cut Broadsword on the Right Diagonal
	8. 虚步藏刀	Hide Broadsword in Empty Step
（五）第四段		Section 4
	1. 旋转扫刀	Rotate and Sweep Broadsword
	2. 翻身劈刀	Turn Over and Cut Broadsword
	3. 缠头箭踢	Wrap Head with Broadsword and Jump-kick
	4. 仆步按刀	Press Broadsword in Crouch Step
	5. 缠头蹬腿	Wrap Head and Drive Leg
	6. 虚步藏刀	Hide Broadsword in Empty Step
	7. 弓步缠头	Wrap Head in Bow Step
	8. 并步抱刀	Join Feet and Hold Broadsword
（六）收势		**Closing Form**

四、初级剑术动作名称
Section IV　Movement Names of Primary Swordplay

（一）起势		**Commencing Form**
	1. 并步侧指	Join Feet and Point Side
	2. 转身前指	Turn Around and Point Forward
	3. 撤步回身	Retreat and Draw Back
	4. 虚步交剑	Change Hands of Sword in Empty Step
（二）第二段		**Section 1**
	1. 弓步直刺	Thrust Straight in Bow Step
	2. 回身后劈	Turn Around and Cut Backward
	3. 弓步平抹	Daub Horizontally in Bow Step
	4. 弓步左撩	Swing Leftward in Bow Step
	5. 提膝平斩	Lift Knee and Cut Horizontally
	6. 回身下刺	Turn Around and Thrust Downward
	7. 挂剑直刺	Hang Up Sword and Thrust Straight

CHAPTER 4 NAMES OF WUSHU ROUTINE

8. 虚步架剑 — Raise Sword in Empty Step
(三) 第二段 — **Section 2**
1. 虚步平劈 — Cut Horizontally in Empty Step
2. 弓步下劈 — Cut Downward in Bow Step
3. 带剑前点 — Bring Sword and Point Forward
4. 提膝下截 — Lift Knee and Intercept Downward
5. 提膝直刺 — Lift Knee and Thrust Straight
6. 回身平崩 — Turn Around and Burst Horizontally
7. 歇步下劈 — Cut Downward in Seated Step
8. 提膝下点 — Lift Knee and Point Downward
(四) 第三段 — **Section 3**
1. 并步直刺 — Join Feet and Thrust Straight
2. 弓步上挑 — Block Upward in Bow Step
3. 歇步下劈 — Cut Downward in Seated Step
4. 右截腕 — Reinforce Right Wrist
5. 左截腕 — Reinforce Left Wrist
6. 跃步上挑 — Block Upward in Jumping Step
7. 仆步下压 — Press Downward in Crouch Step
8. 提膝直刺 — Lift Knee and Thrust Straight
(五) 第四段 — **Section 4**
1. 弓步平劈 — Cut Horizontally in Bow Step
2. 回身后撩 — Turn Around and Swing Up Backward
3. 歇步上崩 — Burst Upward in Seated Step
4. 弓步斜削 — Snick Obliquely in Bow Step
5. 进步左撩 — Step Forward to Swing Leftward
6. 进步右撩 — Step Forward to Swing Rightward
7. 坐盘反撩 — Swing Backward in Crossed-seated Step
8. 转身云剑 — Turn Around and Spin Sword
(六) 收势 — **Closing Form**
1. 虚步持剑 — Hold Sword in Empty Step
2. 并步还原 — Join Feet and Revert

五、初级棍术动作名称
Section V Movement Names of Primary Cudgelplay

（一）起势	**Commencing Form**
1. 并步持棍	Join Feet and Hold Cudgel
2. 提棍上举	Lift Cudgel Upward
（二）第一段	**Section 1**
1. 弓步劈棍	Cut Cudgel in Bow Step
2. 弓步撩棍	Swing Up Cudgel in Bow Step
3. 虚步上拨棍	Poke Cudgel Upward in Empty Step
4. 虚步把拨棍	Poke Cudgel Handle in Empty Step
5. 插步抡劈棍	Swing and Cut Cudgel in Inserting Step
6. 翻身抡劈棍	Turn Over, Swing and Cut Cudgel
7. 马步平抡棍	Swing Cudgel Horizontally in Horse-ride Step
8. 跳步平抡劈棍	Swing and Cut Cudgel Horizontally in Jumping Step
（三）第二段	**Section 2**
1. 单手抡劈棍	Swing and Cut Cudgel with One Hand
2. 提膝把劈棍	Lift Knee, and Cut Cudgel Handle
3. 弓步抡劈棍	Swing and Cut Cudgel in Bow Step
4. 弓步背棍	Back Cudgel in Bow Step
5. 挑把棍	Block Cudgel Handle
6. 转身弓步戳棍	Turn Around and Poke Cudgel in Bow Step
7. 踢腿撩棍	Kick and Swing Up Cudgel
8. 弓步拉棍	Pull Cudgel in Bow Step
（四）第三段	**Section 3**
1. 提膝拦棍	Lift Knee and Block Cudgel
2. 插步抡把劈棍	Swing Cudgel Handle and Cut in Inserting Step
3. 马步抡劈棍	Swing and Cut Cudgel in Horse-ride Step
4. 翻身马步抡劈棍	Turn Over, Swing and Cut Cudgel in Horse-ride Step

5.	上步右撩棍	Step Forward and Block Cudgel on the Right
6.	上步左撩棍	Step Forward and Block Cudgel on the Left
7.	转身仆步摔棍	Turn Around and Throw Cudgel in Crouch Step
8.	弓步崩棍	Burst Cudgel in Bow Step

（五）第四段 **Section 4**

1.	马步把劈棍	Cut Cudgel in Horse-ride Step
2.	坐盘半抡劈棍	Cross Legs Sitting, Swing Semi-circle and Cut Cudgel
3.	左平舞花棍	Left Horizontal Wave-circle Cudgel
4.	右平舞花棍	Right Horizontal Wave-circle Cudgel
5.	插步下点棍	Point Cudgel Downward in Inserting Step
6.	弓步下点棍	Point Cudgel Downward in Horse-ride Step
7.	插步下戳棍	Poke Cudgel Downward in Inserting Step
8.	提膝拦棍	Lift Knee and Block Cudgel

（六）还原式 **Reverting Form**

六、八式太极拳动作名称
Section VI   Movement Names of 8-form Taichi

（一）起势 **Commencing Form**

1.	倒卷肱	Step Back and Whirl on Both Sides
2.	搂膝拗步	Brush Knee and Twist Step
3.	野马分鬃	Part Wild Horse's Mane
4.	云手	Wave Hands like Clouds
5.	金鸡独立	Golden Rooster Stands on One Leg
6.	蹬脚	Kick with Heel
7.	揽雀尾	Grasp Sparrow's Tail
8.	十字手	Cross Hands

（二）收势 **Closing Form**

七、16式太极拳动作名称
Section VII   Movement Names of 16-form Taichi

（一）起势　　　　　　**Commencing Form**
1. 左右野马分鬃　　　Part Wild Horse's Mane on Both Sides
2. 白鹤亮翅　　　　　White Crane Spreads Its Wings
3. 左右搂膝拗步　　　Brush Knee and Twist Step on Both Sides
4. 进步搬拦捶　　　　Step Forward, Deflect (Down), Parry and Punch
5. 如封似闭　　　　　Apparent Close-Up
6. 单鞭　　　　　　　Single Whip
7. 手挥琵琶式　　　　Pipa Strumming Posture
8. 倒卷肱　　　　　　Step Back and Whirl on Both Sides
9. 左右玉女穿梭　　　Fair Lady Works at Shuttles on Both Sides
10. 海底针　　　　　　Needle at Sea Bottom
11. 闪通臂　　　　　　Flash Out Arms
12. 云手　　　　　　　Wave Hands like Clouds
13. 左右揽雀尾　　　　Grasp Sparrow's Tail on Both Sides
14. 十字手　　　　　　Cross Hands
（二）收势　　　　　　**Closing Form**

八、24式太极拳动作名称
Section VIII   Movement Names of 24-form Taichi

（一）起势　　　　　　**Commencing Form**
1. 左右野马分鬃　　　Part Wild Horse's Mane on Both Sides
2. 白鹤亮翅　　　　　White Crane Spreads Its Wings
3. 左右搂膝拗步　　　Brush Knee and Twist Step on Both Sides
4. 手挥琵琶式　　　　Pipa Strumming Posture
5. 倒卷肱　　　　　　Step Back and Whirl on Both Sides

6.	左揽雀尾	Grasp Sparrow's Tail—Left Style
7.	右揽雀尾	Grasp Sparrow's Tail—Right Style
8.	云手	Wave Hands like Clouds
9.	单鞭	Single Whip
10.	高探马	High Pat on Horse
11.	右蹬脚	Heel Kick the Right Side
12.	双峰贯耳	Strike Ears with Both Fists
13.	转身左蹬脚	Turn Body and Kick with Left Heel
14.	左下独立式	Push Down and Stand on One Leg—Left Style
15.	右下独立式	Push Down and Stand on one Leg—Right Style
16.	左右穿梭	Work at Shuttles on Both Sides
17.	海底针	Needle at Sea Bottom
18.	闪通臂	Flash Out Arms
19.	转身搬拦捶	Turn Body, Deflect (Down), Parry and Punch
20.	如封似闭	Apparent Close-Up
21.	十字手	Cross Hands
(二)	收势	**Closing Form**

九、42 式太极拳动作名称
Section IX Movement Names of 42-form Taichi

(一)	起势	**Commencing Form**
1.	右揽雀尾	Grasp Sparrow's Tail—Right Style
2.	左单鞭式	Left Single Whip
3.	提手上式	Lift Hand
4.	白鹤亮翅	White Crane Spread Its Wings
5.	搂膝拗步	Brush Knee and Twist Step
6.	撇身捶	Punch with Fists Aside Before Body
7.	捋挤势	Stroking and Squeezing Posture
8.	进步搬拦捶	Step Forward, Reflect (Down), Parry and Push
9.	如封似闭	Apparent Close-Up
10.	开合手	Opening and Closing of Hands

11.	右单鞭式	Right Single Whip
12.	肘底看捶	Fist under Elbow
13.	转身推掌	Turn Body and Push Palm
14.	玉女穿梭	Fair Lady Works at Shuttle
15.	左右蹬脚	Heel Kicks on Both Sides
16.	掩手肱捶	Cover Hand and Arm with Fist
17.	野马分鬃	Part Wild Horse's Mane
18.	云手	Wave Hands like Clouds
19.	退步打虎	Step Backwards and Beat Tiger
20.	右蹬脚	Kick with Right Leg
21.	双峰贯耳	Punch (Strike) Ears with Both Fists
22.	左分脚	Kick with Left Leg
23.	转身拍脚	Turn Body and Slap Foot
24.	上步栽捶	Step Forward and Punch Downward
25.	斜飞式	Oblique Flying
26.	单鞭下势	Whip Hand Down
27.	金鸡独立	Golden Rooster Stands on One Leg
28.	退步穿掌	Step Backward and Thrust Palm
29.	虚步压掌	Press Palm in Empty Step
30.	独立托掌	Standing on One Leg and Hold Up Palm
31.	马步靠	Lean Sideways in Horse-ride Step
32.	转身大捋	Big Stroke with Body Turn
33.	歇步擒打	Hold and Punch in Seated Step
34.	穿掌下势	Thread Palm and Lowering Movements (Push Down)
35.	上步七星	Step up to Form Seven Stars
36.	退步跨虎	Step Backward and Mount Tiger
37.	转身摆莲	Turn Body with Lotus Kick
38.	弯弓射虎	Draw Bow to Shoot Tiger
39.	十字手	Cross Hands
(二)	收势	**Closing Form**

第五章
CHAPTER 5

一般词汇

GENERAL VOCABULARY

A

爱好者	enthusiast
安稳的	smooth and steady
安神	calm the nerves
按劲	pressing strength
按掌	pressing palm position
暗劲	hidden strength
凹肚	draw in belly
凹胸	pull in chest
拗步	twisted step
拗步冲拳	Thrust Fist in Twisted Step
拗弓步	twisted bow step
拗弓步推掌	Push Out Palm in Twisted Bow Step

B

八段锦	eight-"brocade" exercise; eight-section "brocade" exercise
八方	Eight Directions
八法	eight-skill boxing
八卦连环掌	eight-diagram interlocking palm
八极拳	eight-pole boxing
八极剑	eight-pole swordplay
八十八式太极拳	eighty-eight-form Taichi
八要	Eight Essentials
八字诀	Eight-Character Formula
八字掌	inverted V-shaped palm
拔背	keep one's back straight; strength one's back
拔根	lift heel; raise heel
霸王举鼎	Xiang Yu Lifts Tripod
白鹤亮翅	White Crane Flashes Wings
白蛇吐信	White Snake Shoots Out Tongue; White Snake Spits Tongue
白猿献果	White Ape Presents Fruit

百兵之首	"head" of various weapons
百兵之帅	leader of weapons
百兵之王	king of weapons
摆莲脚	lotus-swing foot position; outward-swinging foot position; swing foot outward
摆脱	escape; undo a hold; unfold a grip
摆脱控制	hold broken
摆掌	swinging palm position; swing palm
拜师	take sb. as one's teacher
搬拦捶	Deflect(Down), Parry and Punch
半决赛	semifinal
半空翻	semi-aerial tumbling
半马步	half horse-ride step
半屈姿势	semi-crouch stance
半身	half body
半圆	half circle
绊摔	lift-over with tripping
膀	arm; shoulder; upper arm
绑	bind
棒	club; cudgel
保镖	bodyguard
保护区	safety area
保健	health protection
保健练习	keep-fit exercise
保持某人的平衡	maintain one's balance; keep one's balance
抱	hold; embrace; lock
抱双腿	double leg-hold
抱虎归山	Embrace Tiger and Return to Mountain
抱起	pick-up
抱拳	holding fist position; hold fists together
抱摔	body slam
抱腿摔	crotch lift
抱球练习	ball-holding exercise

抱双腿摔	double-leg tackle; double-leg pick-up; double-leg drop
抱膝	knee lock
抱掌	encircle with palm; encircling palm position
爆发劲	explosive strength
爆发力	explosive force
背(部)	back
报告员	announcer
报分	auditory scoring
笨拙的	inept
被淘汰	go down
本届冠军	reigning champion
绷	stretch tight; draw tight
绷带	wrapping; bandage
蹦	spring; jump; leap
绷劲	springing strength
鼻梁	bridge of the nose
鼻祖	originator; earlist ancestor
比赛	contest; competition
必修功	required exercise
表情放松	relaxed expression
比赛场地	competition area
比赛大会	meeting
比赛地点	competition site
比赛服装	competition uniform
比赛规则	playing rule
比赛时间	competition time
比赛项目	competition event
比试	have a competition
闭目养神	refresh one's spirit by closing one's eyes
闭气	hold breath; block breath
闭眼	close eyes
臂	arm
臂力	arm strength

避实击虚	avoid the solid and strike at the weak; avoid the strong and strike at the weak
庇身捶	Shield Body with Fist
变幻莫测的	capricious
变换	alternate; vary
鞭拳	whip with fist
表演	performance; demonstration; display
表演太极	perform Taichi
表演项目	performance event
兵器	weaponry; weapon
并步	closed step; bring feet together
掤在两臂	warding rests on both arms
摒除	get rid of; dismiss; discard
屏气	hold breath
摒除杂念	dismiss distracting thoughts
拨草寻蛇	Brush Aside Grass to Search for Snake
拨掌	parrying fist position
波平浪静	Waves Calm Down
不分胜负	draw; deadlock
不偏	not inclined to one side
不相上下	neck and neck; nip and tuck
补充训练	supplementary training
步子	step; stance
步法	step position; footwork
步活	agile in step
步稳如山	step as steady as a mountain
步型	step; step form; step pattern
步与身合	keep step in harmony with body

C

采气	collect one's qi; collect vital energy
裁判	judge; referee
裁判委员会	jury

裁判长	chief referee; head judge
踩八卦	step on the eight diagrams
抄拳	drill boxing
侧空翻	cartwheel
侧面	side; flank
侧面进攻	flank attack
侧平衡	balance stand sideways
侧倾	incline sideward
侧手翻	cartwheel
叉步	crossed step
插	insert; stab
插步	inserting step
插掌	insert palm; inserting palm position
缠绕	wind; twine
缠丝劲	silk-twining strength
场上裁判	referee
朝后指	point backward
朝前指	point forward
朝上指	point upward
朝下指	point downward
撤	draw back
撤步	withdrawal step; withdraw foot
撤身	move body back
陈式太极拳	Chen-style Taichi
陈式太极拳第一路	first-routine Chen-style Taichi
陈氏简化太极拳	simplified Chen-style Taichi
陈氏老/新架太极拳	old-frame/new-frame Chen-style Taichi
陈氏太极剑术/刀术	Chen-style Taichi swordplay/sabreplay
沉肩	sink shoulders; keep shoulders down; loose shoulders
沉髋	lower hips
沉气	sink vital energy
沉稳的	steady
沉着的	calm

持久力	staying power
持久性	durability; endurance
冲拳	rush fist; punch fist; rushing fist position
冲天炮	Punch Upward
重复动作	repetitive movement
抽回	draw back
初级套路	elementary routine
初级太极拳班	elementary Taichi class
初收	First Closing
初学者	beginner
出其不意	take sb. by surprise; catch sb. unaware
出神入化	reach the acme of perfection
出手	skill displayed in making opening moves
踹腿	kick with sole
穿掌	thrust palm; thrusting palm position
传	hand down
传人	successor
传神的	vivid; lifelike
传授	impart; pass on
传统武术	traditional Wushu
传统养生功	traditional health-preservation inner exercise
创始人	founder
垂肩(肘)	droop shoulders
纯熟的	skillful
脆劲	crisp strength; abrupt strength
寸劲	inch strength; explosive strength
催力	exert out strength

D

搭手	hand-joining exercise; join hands
打	strike; hit
打败	beat; defeat
打虎式	Tiger-striking Posture

打破平衡	break a balance
大架	big frame
大开大合	extensive opening and closing
大蟒翻身	Big Boa Turns Over
大腿	thigh
代表队	representative team
单按掌	press single palm
单臂绕环	circle single arm
单鞭	single whip
单鞭下势	Whip Hand Down
单勾手	hook with one hand
单换掌	single-shifting palm (position)
单拍脚	single-slapping foot position; slap single foot
单推手	single-hand-pushing exercise; push single hand
单托掌	single-up-holding palm position; hold up single palm
单项比赛	individual competition; individual event
丹田	dantian (acupoint)
丹田呼吸法	dantian breathing method
当头炮	cannon right overhead
裆	crotch
挡	ward off; block
导引	breathing exercise
导引养生功	daoyin health-preservation exercise
倒卷肱	Step Back and Whirl on Both Sides
倒撵猴	Step Back to Repulse Monkey
道家	Taoist
道教	Taoism
道士	Taoist priest
得分相等	equal marks
蹬脚	kick with heel
低架	lower position; low posture
低头躲闪	bow one's head to evade
底盘	base part

第一届太极拳比赛	the first Taichi match
第一流的	top-class; top-ranking
丁步	T-shaped step; T step
定步推手	push hands with feet fixed; push hands in fixed steps
定步练习	exercise in fixed steps
定式	fixed posture; fixed form
懂劲	know how to interpret energy
动静	motion and stillness
动静分明	clear distinction between motion and stillness
动静结合	combine motion with stillness
动如脱兔,静若处子	move like a galloping hare, and stay quietly as a virgin
动迅静定	move quickly in motion and keep stable in stillness
动作	movement
动作组合练习	combination exercise
动作名称	movement name
抖臂	shake arms
独具一格	have a style of one's own
独具特色	distinctive feature
独立步	stand on one leg
独立平衡	keep balance one leg
独立蹬脚	stand on one leg and kick with heel
独立下式	stand on one leg with crouched step
独立托掌	stand on one leg and hold up palm
独立右蹬脚	stand on one leg and kick with the right heel
段位	rank; grade
锻炼	have physical training; take exercise
锻炼方法	method of training
锻炼效果	result of training
对练	paired practice; dual exercise
对练套路	sparring routine; routine for paired practice
对手	opponent

蹲	squat
度势	judge the situation
多余动作	extra movement
躲	evade
躲避动作	evasive movement
跺脚	stamp

E

恶念	wild thoughts
额头	forehead
峨眉派	Emei school
饿虎扑食	hungry tiger pounces on the prey
儿童组	children group
儿童太极拳	children Taichi
二级裁判员	second-class referee
二级教练员	second-class coach
二级武士	second-grade warrior
二起脚	double kicks
二十四式简化太极拳	twenty-four-form simplified Taichi

F

发放	emit; deliver; release
发放外气功	external-qi-delivery exercise
发劲（力）	exert out strength; strength exertion
发劲动作	strength-exertion movement
发劲方法	strength-exertion method
发力顺达	exert out strength smoothly
发声	utter a shout
发源地	place of origin; birthplace
放松静立式	still-standing relaxation posture
放松疗法	relaxation therapy
放松训练法	relaxation training method
翻花舞袖	Turn Flowers Over and Brandish Sleeves

翻身	turn body up
翻身二起脚	Turn Body Up and Make Double Kicks
翻身右起脚	Turn Body Up to Kick Up the Right Foot
翻掌	turn up palm; up-turning palm position
反复地	again and again
反攻	counter-attack
反关节	lock the joints; joint lock
反击	counter
反擒拿	counter capture
反弹力	rebounding strength
反抓腕	reverse wrist-hold
反复练习	practise again and again
犯规	foul; offence
犯规动作	unnecessary roughness
犯规者	offender
防守	defence; guard
防身术	self-defence art
防守练习	blocking drill; defensive boxing
防守姿势	defensive position; defence position
放松	relax; loosen
肺活量	vital capacity
分脚	separating foot position; separate feet
分级	classification
分开	break
分掌	separating palm position; separate palms
风格	style
风格不同	different in style
风摆荷叶	Wind Sways Lotus Leaves
风扫梅花	Wind Sweeps Away Plum Blossoms
伏地前扫退	Sweep Leg Forward with Hands on Ground
俯身	bend
浮	float
俯身后扫	Bend Body and Sweep Backward

俯卧	lie down on one's stomach
俯卧撑	push-up
辅导中心	coaching center
辅助练习	supplementary exercise
腹部	stomach; abdomen
腹式呼吸法	abdominal respiration (breathing) exercise
副裁判长	deputy chief referee (judge)
负重训练	weight training
附加动作	additional movement

G

盖步	forward-inserting step; insert leg forward
盖掌	thumping palm position
改变动作方向	change the direction of movement
干净、利索的	clean and sharp
刚劲	firm strength; vigorous strength
刚柔的	firm and gentle
高级教练员	senior coach
刚柔并(相)济	combination of firmness and gentleness; combination of hardness and softness
高级阶段	advanced phase
高架	high position (posture)
高难度动作	technically difficult movement
高山流水	Lofty Mountain and Flowing Water
高探马	High Pat on Horse
高虚步	High Empty Step
高与肩平	shoulder height; up to the shoulder level
格挡	parry; block
格斗	wrestle; grapple
个人项目	individual event
个人全能	individual all-round
个人全能比赛	individual all-round competition
个人全能冠军	individual all-round champion

跟步	following step
弓步	bow step
弓背	arch one's back
弓腰	arch one's waist (back)
弓仆步	bow-crouch step
弓腿	bend leg
攻防	defence and attack
攻防技术	defence and attack technique
功防意识	attack and defence consciousness
攻击法	attack method
攻击距离	attack range
攻击距离以内/外	in/out of range
攻守兼备	combine offence and defence
功法	work
功夫	kung fu
功架	boxing posture; position
功力	work power
功效	efficacy
勾	hook
勾手	hook with hand; hooking hand position
股骨	femur
掼拳	sweep fist obliquely upward; sideways-sweeping fist position
规定时间	required time
规定套路	compulsory routine; required routine
规则	rule
跪下	thrust in with the knee
滚翻	roll
滚翻动作	rolling movement
棍	cudgel; stick
国粹	national quintessence; national essence
国家队	national team
国家级裁判员	national referee

国家级教练员	national coach
国际太极拳研讨会	International Taichi Symposium
国技	national skill
国际太极拳邀请赛	International Taichi Invitational Tournament
国术	national arts
国术馆	national arts center
过渡性动作	transitional movement

H

海底针	Insert Needle to Sea Bottom; Needle at Sea Bottom
含胸	draw in chest; bring in chest
含劲	latent force
郝氏太极拳	Hao-style Taichi
合	close; combination; harmony
合腕	close wrists
合膝	press knees inward
合掌	joining palm position; join palms
和尚	monk
鹤立鸡群	Crane Stands Among Crowd of Chickens
黑带	black belt
黑虎掏心	Black Tiger Grabs at Heart
狠的	ruthless
横	swing sideways; poke sideways
横叉	cross-split; straddle split
横裆步	side-crotch step; side step
横劲	sideways strength
喉咙	throat
后叉步	back crossed step
后叉腿低式平衡	inserting-leg-backward low-position balance; low-position balance with leg inserting backward
后扫腿	backward-swinging leg position
后脑	back of head
后退一步	one step backward

后腿蹬地	drive with the rear leg
后倒	back fall
后段	rear section
后丹田	back dantian; mingmen acupoint
后蹬腿	backward-heel-kicking leg position; kick backward with heel
后空翻	backward somersault
后发先至	reach first by striking after an opponent has struck
后发制人	gain mastery by striking only after an opponent has struck
后落	land backward
后手翻	back handspring; flip-flop
后踢腿	Kick Backward
后腿	rear leg
后退	draw back; step back
后天之气	acquired qi
后压腿	press leg behind
后仰	lean backward
后扫腿	backward-sweeping leg position; sweep leg backward
后腰	rear hip throw
呼吸	breathe; breath; respire; respiration
呼吸放松法	breathing relaxation method
呼吸养生法	breathing health-preservation method
呼吸方法	respiratory method
呼吸机能	respiratory function
呼吸系统	respiratory system
呼吸节奏	breathing rhythm
呼气	exhale
弧形	arc; curve
弧形步	curved step; arc step
虎抱头	Tiger Holds Head
虎口	tiger-mouth; hollow between thumb and forefinger
护齿	gum shield

护裆	protector cup; cup protector; protective cup
护具	protector
护膝	knee protector
护胸	shield chest; chest protector
护心捶	shield heart with fist
滑倒	slip-down
滑步	slide step
画圈子	draw circles
化解	dissolve one's grip
化劲	neutralizing strength; neutralize one's oncoming force
踝关节	ankle
还击	counter
还原	Return to Original Posture
缓慢的	slow
缓如鹰	as slow as a wheeling eagle
回合数	round
浑厚的	bold and vigorous; simple and vigorous
活步	moving step
活步推手	moving-step hand-pushing exercise; push hands with moving feet

J

肌肉	muscle
击败	defeat
击倒	knock down
击地捶	Punch Down Towards Ground
脊柱	back bone; spine
脚前掌	sole of foot
基本手型	basic hand form
基本功	basic work; basic training
基本步法	basic step position
基本动作	basic movement
基本姿势	basic posture

基本拳法	basic boxing technique
基本步型	basic step form
基本技法	basic technique (skill)
基本理论	basic theory
基本战术	elementary tactics
集体表演	group performance
集体练习	group exercise
集体项目	group event
挤劲	squeezing strength
继承	inherit
记分裁判	scorekeeper
记分制	point system
记录员	recorder
计时员	timekeeper
技法	fighting skill; fighting art
技击	fighting skill
技击八法	Eight Fighting Skills
技击动作	fighting movement
技击意识	fighting consciousness
技巧(术)	skill; technique
技术训练	technical training
技术要求	technical requirement
技术要领	technical essentials
技术高超	superb skill
夹	clip; lock
夹臂	arm lock; squeeze arms
夹拳	upholding fist position
架	uphold; raise
架打	uphold and punch
架掌	uphold palm
肩臂练习	exercise of shoulders and arms
肩倒立	shoulder stand
肩关节	shoulder joint

肩靠	lean with shoulder
肩与胯合	keep shoulders in harmony with hips
简化太极拳	simplified Taichi
简易擒拿术	simplified capture skill
剑如飞凤	a brandish sword like a flying phoenix
健将	master sportsman
健身	keep one's body healthy; build one's body
健身武术	body-building Wushu
见力化力	neutralize force when meeting force
间接进攻	indirect attack
间歇训练	interval training; intermittent training
僵劲	stiff strength
僵硬的	stiff; rigid
交叉步	crossed step
交换步	change steps; change feet
交流	exchange
交手	fight hand to hand; engage in a hand-to-hand fight
脚背/脚面	back of foot (instep)
脚跟	heel
脚法	footwork; foot position
脚尖点地	toes on the ground
脚尖外撇	toes outward
脚外侧	outer side of foot
脚内侧	inner side of foot
脚与胯合	keep feet in harmony with hips
脚掌	sole
教练	coach; instructor
解脱	break off; loosen a grip
借劲	borrowing strength
接上式	continuing from the previous movement
紧的	tight; tense
劲力	strength
劲力顺达	apply force smoothly

劲敌	challenger
进步栽捶	Step Forward to Punch Down
进步搬拦捶	Step Forward to Deflect (Down), Parry and Punch
进步指裆捶	Step Forward and Punch at Crotch
进步	step forward
进攻	attack
近三退三	three steps forward and three steps backward
进退	advance and retreat
进退自如	advance and retreat very smoothly
近侧	near side
近战	infighting
金刚捣锥	Buddha's warrior attendant
金鸡独立	Golden Rooster Stands on One Leg
精华	quintessence; essence; elite
精神	spirit; vigour
精神集中	concentrate; focus on
精神内守	keep one's spirit in the interior
精髓	quintessence
精武体育会	Jingwu Sports Association
精湛的	perfect; superb; exquisite
颈部紧张	bull neck
警告	warning
静如岳	as static as a mountain
静止的	static; motionless
竞技状态	playing condition
竞技状态良好	in good shape
竞技状态失常	out of shape
竞赛武术	competition Wushu
竞赛项目	competition event
胫骨	tibia
九段	nine grade
纠偏方法	deviation-rectifying method
纠正偏差	rectify deviation

局部发力	partial strength exertion
聚气	accumulate vital energy; gather vital energy
俱乐部比赛	club competition
撅臀	stick up buttock; protrude buttock
绝对胜利	win by a fall
绝对失败	loss on fall
绝对优势	absolute superiority; supremacy
绝技(招)	unique skill
决赛成绩	final result
决赛	final
借力发力	borrow the rival's force and use it against oneself

K

开步站立	stand in open step
开步抱拳	Hold Fist beside Waist in Open Step
开弓	Draw Bow
开合	open and close
开合法	open-and-close method
开合式	open-and-close form
开合运气法	open-and-close qi-circulation method
开呼合吸	exhale in opening while inhaling in closing
开立步	apart step; stand with feet apart
开山鼻祖	earlist founder
开中寓合	contain closing in opening
砍掌	chopping palm position
靠	lean; strike with shoulder
靠劲	leaning strength
靠身	lean body
空手的	bare-handed
空中摆莲	swinging-lotus-in-mid-air skill
空翻	flip; aerial; somersault
控腿	control leg
口授	give verbal instructions

口鼻呼吸法	mouth and nose concurrent-breathing method
扣	press in; draw in
扣腿平衡	pressing-foot-behind-knee balance
枯树盘根	Withered Tree Twists Roots
跨步	striding step
胯	hip
快似闪电	as quick as a flash of lightning
快速连贯的	quick and continuous

L

拉弓射箭式	Draw Bow and Shoot Arrow
来回劲	back-and-forth strength
拦	block
拦雀尾	Grasp Sparrow's Tail
懒扎衣	Lazy about Tying Coat
乱挽花	picking-flowers-freely exercise
老架太极拳	old-frame Taichi
老拳师	Wushu veteran
肋骨	rib
擂台	Wushu ring; ring of martial contests
类别	classification
狸猫上树	Leopard Cat Climbs Up Tree
里合腿	inward-swinging leg position; swing leg inward
里扣	press inward; turn inward
里搂	brush (claws) inward
力劈华山	Split Huashan Mountain in Vertical Circle
立身中正	keep body upright
立腰	keep waist erect
立掌	standing palm
力大脚尖	concentrate force at toes
力点	focus of strength; point of exertion
力量	strength; force; power
力量训练	strength training

力量顺达	smooth exertion of strength; smooth delivery of strength
连贯的	continuous; coherent
连贯动作	consecutive movement
练习方法	training method
练功法	practice method
练习者	practitioner
炼丹家(师)	elixir maker; alchemist
炼丹术	elixir-making art; alchemy
敛臀	pull in buttock; hold back buttock
撩掌	up-swinging fist position
两脚开立	stand with feet apart
两脚平行开立	stand with feet parallel and apart
两脚站立之势	standing-on-both-legs posture
两肩着地	fall; fall down
两仪	Two Principles; yin and yang; negative and positive
亮掌	flashing palm position; flash palm
捌	split
捌劲	splitting strength
灵活的	nimble; agile; flexible
灵活多变	active and diverse
流传	hand down; spread
流派	school; branch; sect
六封似闭	Six Sealings and Four Closings
六合	Six Harmonies; Six Combinations; coordination between the six parts of the human body (namely, hand, elbow, shoulder, foot, knee and hip)
六字诀	six-character formula
搂手	brush hand; brushing hand position
搂手弓步冲拳	Brush Hand and Thrust Fist in Bow Step
搂膝拗步	Brush Knee and Twist Step
搂膝栽捶	Brush Knee and Punch Down

炉火纯青	the stove fire is pure green—perfection in one's skill; reach absolute clarity and purity
抡臂	circle arm; swing arm
螺旋缠绕	twine in spirals
螺旋劲	spiral strength
落步	dropping step; landing step
落地生根	root feet on the ground
落如鹊	land like a magpie
落如叶	land like a leaf

M

马步	horse step; horse-ride step
马步架掌	Raise Palm in Horse-ride Step
马步靠	Lean Sideways in Horse-ride Step
马步架打	Strike Out One Fist with the Other Upheld in Horse-ride Step
马步右抱球	Hold Ball on the Right in Horse-ride Step
马步右沉腕	Sink Right Wrist in Horse-ride Step
迈步	take a step forward
猫形	cat style
猛的	fierce; powerful; vigorous
绵拳	continuous boxing
民族体育	national sports
敏捷的	agile; nimble; quick
明劲	open strength
抹	wipe; draw back in an arc
抹掌	wiping palm position; wipe with palm
拇指	thumb
木人桩	wooden-man pilework

N

耐力	endurance; staying power
耐力训练	endurance training

南派	southern school
南京中央国术管	Nanjing Central National Arts Center
南拳	southern boxing; south boxing
男子组	men's group
内动	internal motion
内呼吸	internal breath
内松	internal relaxation
内分泌系统	endocrine system
内家	internal school; inner school
内家拳	internal-school boxing; inner-school boxing
内劲	internal strength; inner strength
内扣	press inward; turn inward
内练一口气	practise vital energy inside
内三合	Three Internal Harmonies
内外合一	keep the inner parts in harmony with the outer ones
内旋	turn inward
内外相合	keep the inner and the outer parts
内脏	internal organs
黏	adhere; stick
黏劲	sticking force
年龄组别	age category
拧	twist; wring
拧身	twist body; twisting body position
拧腰	twist waist
凝神	concentrate one's attention; focus one's attention
扭	wrench; twist
怒的	angry; furious
女运动员	sportswoman
女子组	women's group

O

偶然跌倒	accidental fall

P

拍	slap; clap
拍脚	slap foot; slapping foot position
拍掌	slap with palm; slapping palm position
拍手	slap with hand; slapping hand position
拍打放松功	patting-and-striking relaxation exercise
盘肘	winding elbow position; wind with elbow
判定	decision
判分	awarding of points
炮锤	cannon-punch boxing
劈拳	split with fist
琵琶式	lute-holding stance
撇身捶	Punch with Fists Aside before Body; Cast Down with Fist and Palm
盘腿平衡	cross-legged balance; balance with crossed legs
平衡动作	balance movement
平行步	parallel step
平衡力练习	balance exercise
平局	stand-off
平拳	level fist position; level fist; level boxing
平衡	balance
平衡练习	balance exercise
平托掌	hold up the palm levelly
平圆	horizontal circle
平掌	flat palm
评分裁判员	ringside judge
评委会	jury
破解法	break-away method
仆步	crouch step

Q

弃权	abstain; default

弃权者	abstainer
奇经八脉	eight extra channels
前倾	bend forward
清晰、准确的	clear and accurate
屈肘	bend elbow
全面训练	all-round training
起伏	rise and fall
起如猿	rise like an ape
起势	Beginning Form; Commencing Form
起源	originate
器械练习	exercise with weaponry
气功	qigong
气沉丹田	sink vital energy to dantian; bring qi down to dantian
气与力合	keep vital energy in harmony with strength
前段	front section
前俯(倾)	bend forward; incline forward
前俯后仰	bend forward and lean backward
前后绕环	rotate forward and backward
前空翻	front flip
前落	land forward
前扫	sweep forward
前上方	front upper side
前提膝平衡	balance by lifting knee in front
前腿	front leg
前下方	front lower side
前招	Forward Move
强身健体	strengthen one's health and keep the body strong
巧劲	ingenious strength
巧拿	ingenious capture
擒拿法	capture skill; capture method
轻功	light work
轻量级	lightweight

躯干	torso; trunk
屈臂	bend arm
屈伸	bend and stretch
屈伸动作	bending and stretching movement
屈肘	bend elbow
拳	fist
拳理	Wushu theory; boxing theory
拳论	views on Wushu; views on boxing
拳面	face of fist; fist face
拳谱	boxing manual; boxing chart
拳师	Wushu master; boxer
拳术	boxing skill; Chinese boxing
拳型	fist form
拳眼	fist eye; eye of fist
拳谚	Wushu proverb
拳种	boxing category; boxing school
全蹲	full squat; squat fully down
全国冠军	national champion
全国青少年武术运动会	National Teenagers Wushu Sports Meet
全国少数民族运动会	National Minority Nationalities Sports Meet
全国太极拳推手比赛	National Competition of Taichi Hand-pushing Exercise
全国体育学院武术邀请赛	National Wushu Invitational Tournament of Physical Culture Institutes
全国武术比赛	National Wushu Competition; National Wushu Contest
全国武术表演赛	National Wushu Exhibition Match
全国武术观摩交流大会	National Wushu Emulation and Exchange Meeting
全国武术邀请赛	National Wushu Invitational Tournament
全国武术运动会	National Wushu Sports Meet
全面训练	all-round training
雀地龙	Dragon on Ground

R

桡骨	radius
绕臂	arm circling
认输	throw in the sponge
韧带	ligament
柔和的	gentle; soft
柔化	neutralize gently
柔劲	gentle strength
柔中有刚	contain firmness in gentleness
如封似闭	Apparent Close-Up; Seeming Close-Up
如此反复	do this repeatedly
入静	attain tranquility; reach the state of tranquility

S

三换掌	Change Palms Thrice
三级裁判员	third-class referee
三体势	three-part posture
丧失比赛能力	inability to box
扫堂腿	sweeping leg position; sweep leg
闪躲灵活	shifty
闪通背	Flash the Back
闪通臂	Flash Out Arms
擅长	be expert in; be skilled in; be good at
上臂	upper arm
上步	advance step; step up
上步搬拦捶	Step Up to Deflect (Down), Parry and Punch
上步七星	Step Up to Form Seven Stars
上步擒打	Step Up to Capture and Strike
上浮	press (cudgel end) up
上腹部	upper abdomen
上盘功夫	upper-part kung fu
上体前俯	bend the trunk forward

上身	upper body
上肢	upper limb
上肢运动	upper-limb exercise
少数民族武术	minority-nationality Wushu
少林武术学校	Shaolin Wushu School
少林拳	Shaolin boxing
少年组	juvenile group; junior group
身法	body position; body movement
身体平衡	body balance
身轻如燕	body as light as a swallow
身体竖直	keep body straight
身械不协调	body and weapon do not coordinate
身体素质	physical quality; physical attribute
身体姿势	body posture
伸展活动	stretching exercise
神经中枢	nerve center
神经系统	nerve system
神与意合	keep spirit in harmony with mind
升级	promotion
失传	not handed down from past generations
十字摆莲	Swing Lotus with Single Hand; Cross Hands and Swing Leg
十字手	cross hands
使力点落空	neutralize the opponent's force point
使肌肉放松	relax muscles
实腹	keep stomach solid; fill abdomen with vital energy
实战	actual combat
食指	index finger
世界锦标赛	world championships
示范动作	demonstration movement
示范讲解	demonstration and explanation
收	draw back; withdraw; contract
收颌	draw in chin; pull in chin

收胯/腹	draw in hips/belly
收拳	draw back fist; withdraw fist
收势	Closing Posture; Concluding Posture
手背	back of hand
手到眼到	the eyes follow the movements of hands
手法	hand position; hand technique
手法练习	exercises of hand position
手挥琵琶	play the pipa; strum the pipa
手型	hand form
手与脚合	keep hands in harmony with feet
授艺	instruct one's skill
熟练的	skilled; adept
竖叉	sidesplit; regular split
甩臂	swing arm
涮腰	circle trunk; trunk circling
双摆莲	Sweep Leg with Both Hands
双换掌	shift both palms
双手如抱球	both hands as if embracing a ball
双脚分开与肩同宽	feet shoulder-width apart
双手叉腰	put your hands on your waist
双推手	push both hands
双震脚	shake both feet
顺步	natural step
四六步	four-six step
四击合法	combination of the four fighting techniques
四两拨千斤	use four ounces to deflect a thousand pounds; overcome a weight of one thousand catties by four ounces
四正推手	four-due-direction hand-pushing exercise
松活的	relaxed and flexible
耸肩	shrug shoulders
碎步	broken step
缩脖子	draw in neck

缩肩	draw back shoulders
锁骨	collarbone
舒筋活络	relax the muscle and stimulate the blood circulation
上体前倾	bend trunk forward
兽头式	beast head posture

T

塌肩	sink shoulders
塌腰	arch one's back
踏步	tread step
台上裁判员	referee; third man in the ring
台下裁判员	judge; ringside judge
抬腿	raise leg
太极	Taichi; Supreme Ultimate
太极刀术	Taichi saberplay
太极剑术	Taichi swordplay
太极起势	Taichi beginning form
太极球	Taichi ball
太极拳	taijiquan; taiji; Taichi chuan; taichichuan; Taichi; shadow-boxing
太极拳爱好者	Taichi enthusiast
太极拳发源地	birthplace of Taichi
太极拳辅导站	Taichi coaching center
太极拳团体	Taichi organization
太极拳学说	doctrine of Taichi
太极拳之乡	home of Taichi
太极拳训练班	Taichi training class
太极拳研究会	Taichi research association
太极拳运动	Taichi sport
太极拳组织	Taichi organization
太极十三式	thirteen-form Taichi
太极图	Taichi chart
太极推手	Taichi hand-pushing exercise

太极五星捶	Taichi five-star-punch boxing
弹	spring
弹抖劲	springing-shaking strength
弹簧劲	spring strength
弹拳	spring fist; springing fist position
弹跳力	jumping ability
探海平衡	sea-searching balance
探肩	stretch shoulders
探身	stretch body forward
淘汰	eliminate
淘汰赛	elimination game
淘汰制	elimination system
套路名称	routine name
套路	routine; sequence; series; pattern
腾空摆莲	swing lotus in flight
提腹	lift stomach
提肛	lift anus
提裆	lift crotch
提气	lift vital energy
提手	lift hand
提手上势	Hand-Lifting Posture; Lift Hand and Step Up
提膝勾手	Hook Hand with Knee Raised
提膝平衡	balance with knee raised
体格	physique
体能	physical efficiency
体质	physique; constitution
体重分级	weight devision
体随势变	the body positions change along with the postures
跳步	jump step
调整姿势	adjust one's position
跳跃练习	leaping exercise
跳跃动作	leaping movement; jumping movement
贴劲	adhering strength

贴身靠	approach and lean with body
听劲	sense the on-coming force
停止比赛	no contest
挺胯	thrust hips out
挺胸	throw out chest; thrust chest forward
挺胸立腰	thrust chest forward and keep waist erect
同时	at the same time (simultaneously)
同时动作	simultaneous movement
偷步	backward-inserting step
偷梁换柱	Steal Beams and Replace Pillars
头向上顶	hold head upright; keep head upright
突臀	stick out buttock
徒手对练	bare-handed sparring exercise
徒手套路	bare-handed routine
徒手练习	bare-handed exercise
团体冠军	team champion
团体赛	team competition
团体项目	team event
臀部	buttock
推手	hand-pushing exercise
推掌	pushing palm position; push palm
腿法	leg technique; leg movement
腿劲	leg strength
退步	retreat step; step back
退步打虎	Step Back to Strike Tiger; Retreat to Hit Tiger
退步跨虎	Step Back to Ride Tiger
退步收势	Move Back and Return to Original Posture
退出比赛	out of the game
吞吐劲	drawing-stretching strength
托	hold (up)
托气	hold vital energy
托掌	up-holding palm position; hold up palm

W

外摆	outward-swinging leg position; swing (leg) outward
外摆莲	swing leg outward; swing lotus outward
外家拳	external-school boxing; outer-school boxing
外练筋骨皮	do sinew, bone and skin exercise outside
外搂	brush (claws) outward
外撇	turn outward
外三合	Three External Harmonies; Three Outer Harmonies
外旋	turn outward; twist outward
外展	stretch outward; turn outward
弯弓射虎	Bend Bow to Shoot Tiger
腕部擒拿术	wrist capture skill
挽花	trip with front-and-sleeve grip
腕关节	wrist joint
腕力	wrist strength
望月平衡	moon-watching balance
威震八方	Inspire Awe in Eight Directions
微屈肘	bend the elbow slightly
文化遗产	cultural heritage
稳如磐石	as steady as a huge rock
稳如平地	as steady and immovable as the dry land itself
稳扎稳打	play safe
握拳姿势	fist position
吴氏太极拳	Wu-style Taichi
无名指	third finger; ring finger
五步拳	five-step boxing
五脏六腑	internal organs of the human body
武德	Wushu morals
武林	Wushu circles
武僧	boxing monk
无氧训练	anaerobic training
武术爱好者	Wushu enthusiast

武术比赛项目	Wushu competition event
武术表演项目	Wushu performance event
武术初级套路	elementary Wushu routine
武术大师	great master of Wushu
武术代表团	Wushu delegation
武术分类	classification of Wushu
武术高手	Wushu master-hand
武术功底	basic Wushu repertoire
武术馆	Wushu center; martial arts center
武术行家	Wushu expert
武术集训队	Wushu training team
武术家	Wushu master; Wushu artist
武术简史	brief history of Wushu
武术界	Wushu circles
武术竞赛规则	rules for Wushu competition
武术名家	famous Wushu expert; famous Wushu player
武术前辈	Wushu veteran
武术全能冠军	all-round Wushu champion
武术入门	ABC of Wushu
武术史学家	Wushu historian
武术世家	old and well-known family of Wushu
武术套路	Wushu routine
武术特点	characteristic of Wushu
武术遗产	Wushu heritage
武术运动员	Wushu player; Wushu performer
武坛	Wushu world; Wushu circles
武童级	Wushu-child grade
武英级	Wushu-hero grade; martial-hero grade

X

膝关节	knee joint
西南	southwest
习武者	Wushu practitioner

系统训练	systematic training
下对脚尖	face the tiptoe in the lower part
下腹部	lower abdomen
下盘功夫	lower-part skill
下颌微收	chin dropped slightly
下身	lower part of body
下势	down-pushing posture; push down
下肢	lower limb
下肢运动	lower-limb exercise
先发制人	gain mastery by striking first; get the upper hand by taking the initative
掀脚	lift foot; lift sole
相持姿势	neutral position
向前平看	look forward levelly
向前下潜	fold
向上格挡	parry upward
向右移步	right step
象形取意	imitate the form and adopt the meaning
象形拳	imitative boxing
消化系统	digestive system
消极性	passivity
小腹	underbelly
小拇指	little finger
小擒打	Small Capture and Strike
小腿	shank; lower leg
小指侧	edge of palm; small finger side
小周天	small complete revolution
效果	impression; result
歇步	seated step
斜飞式	Oblique-Flying Form; Diagonal Flying
斜劲	oblique strength
斜拦雀尾	Grasp Sparrow's Tail Obliquely
斜身靠	Incline Body and Lean Forward

斜向上	slantingly upward
斜行拗步	Walk Obliquely and Twist Step
协调	coordinate
新陈代谢	metabolism
心动行随	the posture follows the mind
心肺功能	function of heart and lungs
心合于意	combine heart with mind
心静体松	tranquility in mind and relaxation in body
心理训练	psychological training
心神合一	keep heart and spirit at one
心血管系统	cardiovascular system
心与意合	keep heart in harmony with mind
形神合一	keep form and spirit at one
行云流水	floating clouds and floating streams
胸	breast; chest
吸气	inhale
修身	cultivate one's moral character
修身养性	cultivate one's mind and improve one's character
虚的	empty; hollow; void
虚步	empty step; hollow step; suspended step
虚晃	feint
虚劲	insubstantial strength; void strength
虚实的	false and real; void and solid; empty and solid
虚拳	fake blow
虚实相间	alternate emptiness with solidness
蓄劲	accumulate strength
蓄气	accumulate vital energy
旋	revolve; whirl
旋转劲	revolving strength
选拔赛	selective trial; try-out
选手	player; contestant
血液循环	blood circulation
循环	circulate; cycle

循环系统	circulatory system
训练场地	training ground
训练量	volume of training
训练项目	training event

Y

压肩	press shoulders
压腿	press leg
亚军	runner-up; second-place finisher; silver medallist
延长时间	overtime
延年益寿	lengthen one's life
研究会	research association
演习堂	practice arena
眼法	eye position; eye movement
眼神	eye expression; expression in one's eyes
眼睛随视双掌	eyes follow both palms
眼睛向前平视	eyes look straight (forward)
眼与心和	keep eyes in harmony with heart
掩护	cover
掩手肱捶	Cover Hand and Arm with Fist
燕式平衡	swallow-style balance; front horizontal scale
以小打大	achieve maximum result with minimum effort
养生之道	the way to keep in good health
仰身	bend body backward
仰卧起坐	sit-up
仰身平衡	leaning-body-backward balance
腰部	waist; low back
腰部练习	exercise of waist
腰侧	side of waist
腰劲	waist strength
腰椎	lumbar vertebra
腰似蛇行	the waist moves like a crawling snake
要害部位	vital part of body

腰似摆柳	the waist swings like a swaying willow
腰似转轴	waist like a resolving axle
要领	essentials
腋窝	armpit
野马分鬃	Part Wild Horse's Mane; Separate Wild Horse's Mane
业余爱好者	amateur
业余武术学校	amateur Wushu school
一动无有不动	a single movement sets the whole body moving
一级裁判员	first-class referee
医疗	medical treatment
乙组	Group B
以动制静	subdue tranquility with motion
以柔克刚	subdue firmness with softness
以横破道	horizontal force can break vertical force
以快打慢	attack slowness with quickness
以静待动	wait quietly for a moving opponent
以力化力	counteract force with force
以柔化刚	neutralize firmness by softness
以手臂挡开来拳	parry
以小制大	counter a big force with a small one
以腰为轴	use waist as an axle
以意行气	guide vital energy with mind
以肩阻挡	shoulder block
意念法	mind-training skill
意识	consciousness; mind
意守丹田	concentrate mind on dantian
意形合一	integrate mind with posture
意识训练	awareness training
意与气和	keep mind in harmony with vital energy
阴阳	negative and positive; yin and yang
阴阳图	the symbol of yin and yang
阴阳学说	yinyang theory; theory of positive and negative forces

硬功	hard work
用力呼气	exhale deeply
优势	superiority
由松入柔	from relaxation to gentleness
友谊赛	friendship match; friendly match
有氧训练	aerobic training
右擦脚	Rub with Right Foot
右单鞭	Right Single Whip
右蹬脚	Kick with Right Heel
右拍脚	Slap Right Foot
右琵琶式	Strum Pipa—Right Style
右仆步	right crouch step
右下势独立	Push Down and Stand on One Leg—Right Style
右上方	right upper side
鱼跃前滚翻	flying roll-up
与鼻平	at nose level
与肩同高	as high as shoulder
与肩同宽	shoulder width apart
玉女穿梭	Fair Lady Works at Shuttle
预备势	preparatory posture
预备姿势	starting position
预赛	preliminaries; preliminary contest
圆	circle
圆弧步	arc step
圆形动作	circular movement
云手	Wave Hands like Clouds
运动员	player; athlete; sportsman
有利位置	advantageous position
运劲如抽丝，	apply power as if drawing silk from a cocoon,
迈步如猫行	and walk the steps of a cat

Z

砸拳	pounding fist position

再收	Second Closing
栽拳	downward-punching fist position
自选拳	optional boxing
自然门	natural boxing
自然深呼吸	deep and natural breathing
扎实的	solid
站如松	stand like a pine
掌	palm
掌背	back of palm; palm back
掌根	root of palm; base of palm
掌型	palm form
赵堡架太极	Zhaobao-frame Taichi
整劲	whole strength
整体发力	integral strength exertion
正面进攻	frontal attack
正踢腿	frontal kick
支撑腿	supporting leg
直背	keep one's back erect
指裆捶	Hit Crotch with Fist
指关节	knuckle
中国传统武术	traditional Chinese Wushu
中国武术史	Chinese Wushu history
中架	medium frame; medium position
中枢神经系统	central nervous system
中央国术馆	Central National Arts Centre
中正的	upright
中指	middle finger
仲裁委员会	jury; jury of appeal
重心	center of gravity
重心转移	shifting of weight
重如铁	as heavy as iron
周身协调	coordinate various parts of the body
肘底捶	Punch under Elbow

肘与膝合	keep elbows in harmony with knees
主要部位	main part of body
主要流派	major school
主宰于腰	dominated by waist
转换	shift; change
转腰	turn waist
转腰化解	turn the waist to neutralize
转身摆莲	Swing Leg with Body Turn
转腕旋膀	wrist rotation and arm circling
转身大捋	Big Stroke with Body Turn
转身蹬脚	turn the body to kick with heel
桩	keep-push with belt-and-sleeve grip
桩功	stake work
坠肩	drop shoulders
准备活动	warm-up exercise
着力点	striking point
自卫能力	ability of self-defence
自然呼吸	natural breathing; breathe naturally
自我放松训练	self-relaxation training
自选套路	optional routine
宗师	master; master of great learning and integrity
综合训练	combined training
总教练	head coach
总分	aggregate score
纵劈叉	side split
走架子	walking posture
走马观花	View Flowers on Horseback
组合练习	combination exercise
阻挡	blocking
最优秀的运动员	top player
醉拳	drunken boxing
左擦脚	Rub with Left Foot
左弓步	left bow step

左前方	left front side
左后方	left back side
左上方	left upper side
左式	left form; left stance
左推掌	Push Left Palm
左虚步	left empty step
左歇步	left seated step
左摇右晃	Sway to the Left and Right
左右穿梭	Work at Shuttles on Both Sides
左右倒撵猴	Step Back and Repulse Monkey on Both Sides
左右分脚	Separate Instep Kicks on Both Sides
左右野马分鬃	Part Wild Horse's Mane on Both Sides
左右开弓	Draw Bow on the Left and Right
左右转换	alternating left and right
左右金鸡独立	Golden Rooster Stands on One Leg
左右搂膝拗步	Brush Knee and Twist Step on Both Sides
左右压肩	Press Shoulders on Both Sides
坐井观天	Sit in Well to Look at Sky
坐胯	sit hips down
坐盘	cross-legged sitting
坐腕	sit wrist down

第六章
CHAPTER 6

武术专业词汇

WUSHU SPECIFIC WORDS

CHAPTER 6　WUSHU SPECIFIC WORDS
第六章　武术专业词汇

一、手型　Hand Forms

拳	fist
掌	palm
柳叶掌	willow palm
八字掌	finger-palm
勾	hook

二、手法　Hand Positions

抱拳	hold fists together
冲拳	punch fist
架拳	raise fist
栽拳	punch down
抄拳	swing up fist
劈拳	cut fist
格拳	parry fist
上格拳	parry fist up
下格拳	parry fist down

三、掌法　Palm Positions

架掌	raise palm
亮掌	flash palm
推掌	push palm
砍掌	cut palm
按掌	press palm
撤掌	withdraw palm
撩掌	swing up palm
搂手	brush hand
舞花手	circle with arms crossed
十字手	cross hands

云手	Wave Hands like Clouds
勾手	hooking hand position

四、肘法 Elbow Positions

顶肘	push elbow
盘肘	bend elbow
架肘	raise elbow
格肘	parry elbow
横击肘	cross-cut elbow

五、步型 Step Forms

并步	feet together
弓步	bow step
马步	horse-ride step
仆步	crouch step
虚步	empty step
歇步	seated step
坐盘	cross-legged sitting position
丁步	T-shaped step
插步	inserting step
蹲歇步	crouch and seated step
后点步	backward pointing step
跪步	kneeling step
横裆步	side-crotch step

六、步法 Step Positions

击步	hitting step
垫步	hopping step
弧形步	arc step

七、肩功 Shoulder Movements

压肩	shoulder stretching
正压肩	forward shoulder stretching
反压肩	backward shoulder stretching
坐肩	sit on the shoulder
踩肩	step on the shoulder
单臂绕环	single arm circle
双臂绕环	double arms circle
左右绕环	left and right arms circle
交叉绕环	crossed arms circle
抡臂	swing arm
仆步抡拍	swing arms and pat floor in crouch step
抡臂拍脚	swing arms to tap leg

八、腰功 Waist Movements

俯腰	bend down waist
甩腰	bend body forward and backward
涮腰	circle trunk
翻腰	turn waist over
下腰	back back; bend backward into a bridge

九、腿功 Leg Movements

压腿	leg stretching
正压腿	forward leg stretching
侧压腿	side leg stretching
后压腿	backward leg stretching
弓步压腿	stretch leg in bow stance
仆步压腿	stretch leg in crouch step
搬腿	leg lifting

正搬腿	forward leg lifting
侧搬腿	side leg lifting
后搬腿	backward leg lifting
劈腿	leg splitting
竖叉	sidesplit
横叉	cross-splitting
踢腿	kick leg
直摆性腿法	straight-swinging leg position
十字腿	cross-form kick
侧踢腿	side kick
里合腿	kick-circle inward leg
外摆腿	swing leg outward
屈伸性腿法	kick with lower leg
弹腿	spring leg
侧弹腿	side spring leg
蹬腿	drive leg
前蹬	drive forward
后蹬	drive backward
踹腿	kick with sole
侧踹腿	side kick with sole
高踹腿	high kick with sole
低踹腿	low kick with sole
铲腿	shovel leg
扫转性腿法	sweeping-rotating leg position
前扫	forward sweeping
后扫	backward sweeping
击响性腿法	hit sound leg position
单拍脚	slap single foot
斜拍脚	cross-slap foot
里合拍脚	kick-circle inward slap foot
摆莲拍脚	swing lotus and slap foot
直摆性腿法	swing stretched leg
正踢腿	frontal kick

十字腿	cross leg position
侧踢腿	side kick
里合腿	kick-circle inward
外摆腿	kick-circle outward
后撩腿	swing leg backward
前拍脚	front tap foot
里合击响	kick-circle inward with tap foot
外摆击响	kick-circle outward with tap foot
屈伸性腿法练习	kick with lower leg
弹体冲拳	Spring Body and Punch Fist
蹬腿推掌	Kick Heel and Push Palm
侧弹	spring sideward
侧踹腿	side sole kick
抡臂拍脚	Swing Arm and Tap Foot
仆步穿掌	Pierce Palm in Crouch Step
叉步翻腰	Turn Waist Over in Crossed Step
抡臂翻腰	Swing Arm and Turn Waist Over
前扫腿	front sweep
后扫腿	back sweep
弧形步	arc step
跳跃动作练习	jumping exercise
起跳	taking-off
马步翻身跳	turn body over in horse-ride step
摆莲起跳	jumping outside kick
大跃步前窜	giant leap
旋风脚	whirlwind foot
腾空外摆莲	kick-flight as a waving lotus
旋子	butterfly
转体360°	turn body 360°

十、桩功 Stake Stances

马步桩	horse-ride stake stance

弓步桩	bow stake stance
虚步桩	empty stake stance
一字桩	one word stake

十一、跳跃　Jumping Movements

腾空飞脚	jump up to fly foot
旋风脚	whirlwind foot
腾空摆莲	swing lotus in flight
转体360°	turn body 360°

十二、平衡　Balancing

提膝平衡	lift knee balance
燕式平衡	swallow style balance
扣腿平衡	buckle-legged balance
盘腿平衡	cross-legged balance
俯身平衡	bend body balance

十三、跌扑滚翻　Tumbling and Rolling Movements

抢背	forward roll
鲤鱼打挺	carp straightens itself up
乌龙绞柱	black dragon coils around pillar
侧空翻	side somersault
旋子	butterfly
腾空蹬腿	kick with heel in flight

十四、基础动作　Basic Movements

并步抱拳	Join Feet with Fists at the Waist
并步亮拳	Flash Palm in Joining Feet
开立步双冲拳	Punch Fist in Shoulder-width Stance

弓步推掌	Push Palm in Bow Step
弓步上冲拳	Punch Upward in Bow Step
拗弓步冲拳	Punch Fist in Twisted Bow Step
马步冲拳	Punch Fist in Horse-ride Step
仆步架打	Strike Out One Fist with the Other Upheld in Crouch Step
仆步穿掌	Penetrate Palm in Crouch Step
仆步亮掌	Flash Palm in Crouch Step
虚步挑掌	Stick Up Palm in Empty Step
高虚步挑掌	Stick Up Palm in High Empty Step
高虚步上冲拳	Punch Fist Upward in High Empty Step
歇步盖打	Thump Down Seated Step
插步双摆拳	Circle Both Palms in Inserting Step
坐盘插掌	Thrust Palm in Cross-legged Sitting
弹踢冲拳	Snap Kick and Punch Fist
弹踢推掌	Snap Kick and Punch Palm
提膝穿掌	Lift Knee and Penetrate Palm
提膝亮掌	Lift Knee and Flash Palm
提膝仆步穿掌	Lift Knee and Penetrate Palm in Crouch Step
击步挑掌	Stick Up Palm in Hitting Step
弧形步亮掌	Flash Palm in S-step
抬头亮掌	Raise Head and Flash Palm
左右勾手	hook with hand on both sides
转身抡臂	Turn Body to Swing Arms in Circle
腾空飞脚	jump up to fly foot
旋风脚	whirlwind foot
腾空摆莲	swing lotus in flight

十五、拳术动作名称 Movement Names of Boxing

按掌	press palm
拗步	twist step
八法(手、眼、身、步、	eight points (hands, eyes, body, step, spirit,

精神、气、力、功）	qi, strength, skills）
摆腿	swing leg
抱球	ball-holding gesture
抱拳礼	hold-fist salute
并步摆拳	Bring Feet Together and Swing Fist
并步击拳	Bring Feet Together and Thrust Fist Forward
并步托掌	Bring Feet Together and Push Up Palm
并步双摆掌	Bring Feet Together and Swing Both Palms
并步刺剑	Thrust Sword with Feet Together
并步点剑	Point Sword with Feet Together
并步对拳	bring feet together and thrust draw fists
并步分掌	Separate Palm with Feet Together
并步举掌	Raise Palm with Feet Together
并步平刺	Trust Horizontally with Feet Together
并步握拳	Stand with Feet Together and Clench Hands into Fists
侧步	sidestep
侧撑	cross support
侧弓步；横裆步	side step
侧空翻转体	cartwheel with body turn
侧立	cross-stand
侧踢腿	kick sideways with leg
侧摔	fall sideways
鱼跃	fish leaping
插手	insert hand
插掌	insert palm
缠腿	twist legs
铲腿	kick sideways with outer edge of foot
朝天蹬	kick upward with heel
撑掌	prop with palm
沉肩垂肘	shoulder low and elbow loose
驰顶	neck held erect without strain
出手	skill displayed in making opening moves

CHAPTER 6 WUSHU SPECIFIC WORDS
第六章 武术专业词汇

踹腿	kick sideways with sole leading
空拳	shadow boxing
捶打	hammer blow
垂肘	hang elbow down
大跃步前穿	jump forward with a long step
单臂侧手翻	one-army cartwheel
单臂倒立	one-army balance
击步	beat step
单脚跳	hop
前手翻	forward handsring
后撩腿	swing leg backward
垫步	skip step
跌叉	fall split
跌扑滚翻	tumble and roll
顶肘	push elbow
独立撑掌	Stand on One leg and Prop Up Palm
翻腕	turn over wrist
反肘关节动作	twisting hammerlock
高虚步亮掌	Flash Palm in High Empty Step
弓步按掌	Press Palm in Bow Step
弓步抱拳	Hold Fists Before Chest in Bow Step
钩脚	hook foot
跪立	kneel sitting
滚肘	rotate elbow
里合腿	kick-circle inward leg
横步	sidestep
横拳	poke fist sideways
后摆	swing backward
后穿	thrust palm backward
后退步	backward step
虎形	tiger form
挤	push; press forward
夹头	head lock

夹腿	leg lock
夹腕	wrist lock
脚跟转向里	turn heel inward
脚尖里扣	turn toe inward
脚尖伸直	point toe straight
进步撩掌	Step Forward to Swing Palm
空中换腿	change of legs during flight
扣腿	ankle pick
鲤鱼打挺	carp straightens itself up
立拳	standing fist
连踢	serial kicks
连续冲拳	serial blows
连续拳	combination blow
两腿并拢	legs together
两脚平立	parallel stance
两肘松垂	keep elbows loose and downward
踉跄步	faltering steps; totter
撩拳	swing up palm
搂掌	brush palm
搂膝拗步	Brush Knee in Twisted Step
鹿形(五禽戏之四形)	deer form (the fourth of the five-animal exercises)
抢背	forward somersault; throw forward with back
拿	catch
内侧格挡	inside parry
鸟形(五禽戏之五形)	bird form (the fifth of the five-animal exercises)
碾步	pivot on ball of foot
望月平衡	moon-watching balance
拍脚顶肘	Slap Foot and Push Elbow
盘腿跌	cross-legged fall
炮拳	punch forward
劈掌	split with palm
劈叉	split
劈叉收腿	leg slide from split

CHAPTER 6　WUSHU SPECIFIC WORDS
第六章　武术专业词汇

撤拳	backward punch
平行步	basic stance
扑虎	catch the tiger; pound on the tiger
起动	start
前臂格挡	forearm block
前冲	punch forward
前倒	fall with face down
前点步	forward step with toes landing on floor
前顶	thrust the elbow forward
前俯压腿	press the leg while bending the trunk forward
前滚翻	forward roll
前控腿平衡	balance and control the leg in front
前劈拳	cut forward with the fist
提膝平衡	front/side knee-lifted balance
前推掌	push the palm forward
前旋	forward rotation
蜻蜓点水	the dragonfly skims the surface of the water
屈伸	flexing and stretching
卧云平衡	lying-on-cloud balance
屈体滚翻	piked roll
屈膝	bending of knee
绕臂	circle arms
如封似闭	apparently close-up
三击	three punches
三型（手型、身型、步型）	three forms (hand form, body form, step form)
前扫腿	upright front sweep
后扫腿	ground and backward sweep
扫转性腿法	circle leg sweep
闪通臂	flash out arms
上步	step forward
上步冲拳	step forward and thrust fist
上勾拳	upper cut
上体后仰	rock-back

上体左转	trunk turns to the left
身法	body position
身体闪躲	dodge
身体竖直	body erects
身体旋转	body rotation
十字手	cross hands
实步	solid step
收腹	contract the abdomen; draw in the abdomen
收势	recovery of the leg; withdraw the leg
收臀	buttocks in; buttocks tucked in
手臂动作	arm action; arm motion; arm movement
手挥琵琶	hand strums the lute
手心向里	palm faces inward
手心向外	palm faces outward
手心向上	palm faces up
手心向下	palm faces down
手型	hand form
竖叉	perpendicular split
摔倒	fall; throw down
双峰贯耳	punch (strike) ears with both fists
双手抓握	double grip
四法(手、身、步、腿法)	four positions (hand, body, foot and leg positions)
四击	four blows
松胯	relax thigh
松拳	open fist
松腰	relax waist
耸肩	shrug shoulder
踏跳步	hurdle
抬腿	lift leg
抬肘	elbow out
太极步法	Taichi-step position
太极推手	Taichi hand-pushing exercise
弹腿	leg kicking

CHAPTER 6 WUSHU SPECIFIC WORDS
第六章 武术专业词汇

探海平衡	explore the sea balance
腾空	flight
腾空摆莲	swing lotus in flight
腾空侧踹	kick sideways with sole during flight
腾空踢腿	jump and kick with the heel
腾空蹬踢	flying sole kick; kick with heel in flight
腾空动作	flight part
腾空飞脚	flying kick
腾空后翻	back flip
腾空前翻	front flip
腾空连环飞脚	double kick in flight
腾空转身飞脚	flying kick with twist
踢	kick
提手	lift hands
提手上势	raise hands and step up
提膝亮掌	flash palm while lifting knee; lift knee and flash palm
提膝平衡	balance with one knee raised
提踵	heels lifted off floor; rise on toes
跳步	jump step
跳换步	jump and change the step
跳跃	leap
挺胸	chest out; trust the chest forward
头手倒立	headstand; head balance
推	push
推开	shave aside
推掌	push palm
腿法	leg position
退步	step backward
退步跨虎	retreat and mount the tiger
臀部呈弧形	curved hip; rounded hip
托掌	lift palm
蛙跳	frog jump

外摆腿	king-swing outward
外抱腿	outside crotch-hold
外展动作	arms sideward lift
往下翻掌	pronate hand; pronate palm
握拳	clench fist
握腕	wristlock
乌龙绞柱	dark dragon coils around a column
五禽戏	five-animal exercises
下冲	strike downward
下蹲	crouch; squat
下颌里收	draw the chin inward; pull in the chin
下势	push down
向后移步	back step
向旁闪躲	side-step hide
向前鱼跃	dive forward
向前越步	jump forward
歇步	seated step
歇步亮掌	display palm in seated step
歇步擒拿	catch and hit in seated step
斜飞式	flying oblique
斜搂膝拗步	obliquely brush knee and twist step
斜身靠	lean obliquely
斜线跳跃	obliquely jump
斜线走	move on the diagonals
熊形	bear form
虚步	empty step
虚步按掌	press palm in empty step
虚拳	fake blow
旋子	horizontal circle in the air; spinning
旋子转体	spinning with twist
压掌	press palm
掩手肱捶	Cover Hand and Arm with Fist
燕式平衡	balance stand; single-leg front lever

CHAPTER 6 WUSHU SPECIFIC WORDS
第六章　武术专业词汇

仰身平衡	single-leg back lever
野马分鬃	Part Wild Horse's Mane
游身八卦掌	round body eight-diagram palm
右/左蹬脚	kick with the right/left heel
右/左勾拳	right/left hook
右/左手化弧	circle the right/left hand
鱼跃前滚翻	flying dive roll
玉女穿梭	Fair Lady Works at Shuttle
猿形	ape form
云手	Wave Hands like Clouds
砸拳	strike the palm of one hand with the fist of the other
栽碑	fall forward with the elbow bent
栽拳	downward punch
掌法	palm position
掌与肩平	palm level with the shoulder
正压腿	press the leg by bending the body forward until the mouth touches the toes
振臂	shake arms
振脚上冲拳	stamp foot and thrust up fist
直臂	extend arm; arm straightened
直立举腿平衡	balance with one leg lifted up
直拳	straight blow
直身前扫	the leg sweeps forward with the body erect
直腕	straight wrist
直腿	straight leg
指法	fingers position
中架	middle frame
重心在右/左脚上	weight on the right/left foot
肘底锤	punch underhanded elbow
抓	grab
转脚跟	pivot on the heel
转身摆莲	Swing Leg with Body Turn

转身搬拦捶	turn to strike; parry and punch
转身撇身捶	turn to strike; parry and punch
转身推掌	turn the body and push palms
转身左蹬脚	turn the body to kick with the left heel
转腕	wrist rotation
转腰	turn waist
纵步	skip the step
钻	corkscrew blows
左/右揽雀尾	Grasp Sparrow's Tail—Left/Right Style
左/右下势独立	Push Down and Stand on One Leg—Left/Right Style
左右穿梭	Work at Shuttles on Both Sides
左右野马分鬃	Part Wild Horse's Mane on Both Sides
坐盘	cross-legged sitting position

十六、器械 Weapons

八卦刀	eight-diagram broadsword
八仙剑	eight-fairy sword
鞭	whip
镖	dart
兵器、器械	apparatus; weapon
叉	fork
禅杖	monk's staff
长兵器	long weapon
春秋刀	spring and autumn broadsword
大刀	long scimitar
单鞭	single whip
剑	sword
鞭	nine-section whip
砍刀	chopper
单刀	cutlass; cutlass pair
刀	broadsword; sabre; sword
短兵器	short weapon

盾	shield
峨眉刺	E'mei piercer; E'mei dagger
飞叉	flying fork
飞虹剑	flying-rainbow sword
鬼头刀	devil's head broadsword
棍	cudgel
戟	halberd; halbert
软兵器	flexible weapon; soft weapon
三节棍	three-section cudgel; three-segment cudgel
双节棍	two-section cudgel
蛇剑	snake sword
蛇矛	snake pike
流星锤	meteor hammer
柳叶刀	willow-leaf broadsword
矛	pike
苗刀	sword sprout
弩	crossbow
朴刀	long-hilt broadsword
齐眉棍	eyebrow-high cudgel

十七、拳种 Boxing Categories

八卦掌	eight-diagram boxing
八极拳	eight extremes boxing
查拳	Cha's shadow-boxing
长拳	long boxing
初级拳	primary boxing
地躺拳	lie-on-the-ground boxing
短拳	short-boxing; short-range boxing
福建南拳	Fujian southern-style boxing
佛家拳	Buddhist-style boxing
狗拳	dog-style boxing
鹤顶拳	crane's crown fist

黑虎拳	black-tiger boxing
猴拳	monkey-style boxing
虎鹤双形拳	tiger-crane double-form boxing
虎拳	tiger-style boxing
简化太极拳	simplified shadow-boxing
六合八法	six harmonies and eight methods
六合螳螂拳	six harmony mantis-style boxing
梅花螳螂拳	plum-blossom mantis-style boxing
迷踪拳	delusive art of boxing
南拳	southern-style boxing
炮锤	cannon boxing
劈挂拳	chop-and-parry boxing
七星螳螂拳	seven-start mantis-style boxing
拳术	barehanded exercise; traditional Chinese boxing
少林拳	Shaolin boxing
蛇拳	snake-style boxing
四十八式太极拳	48-form Taichi
太极拳	shadow-boxing; Taijiquan; Taichi
螳螂拳	mantis-style boxing
铁砂掌	exercise of splitting iron sand bags with the palm and the back of the hand
五虎拳	five-tiger boxing
五行拳	five-element boxing
五祖拳	five-ancestor boxing
武当拳	Wudang boxing
象形拳	imitative boxing
小梅花拳	small plum-blossom boxing
心意拳	heart-and-will boxing
形意拳	form-and-will boxing
杨式太极拳	Yang-style shadow-boxing
鹰爪拳	hawk's claw boxing
咏春拳	Yongchun boxing
岳家拳	Yue-style boxing

子母拳	composite boxing
醉拳	drunkard's boxing

十八、器械动作名称　Movement Names of Weapon

舞花棍	wave-circle cudgel
绞棍	twist cudgel
绞剑	twist sword
截棍	poke cudgel
抱棍	hold cudgel
抱刀	hold broadsword
背花	circle broadsword over the back
并步刺剑	thrust sword with feet together
并步点剑	point sword with feet together
拨棍	poke with cudgel
拨刀	poke with broadsword
单刀进枪	single broadsword against spear
对打	clash; encounter
空手对刀枪	bare-handed fight against broadsword and dagger
空手夺匕首	empty hands against dagger
双刀进枪	double broadsword against spear
双手剑	play a sword with double hands
藏刀	hide the broadsword
侧劈	cut sideways
缠	coil
穿剑	thrust sword
穿梭棍	shuttle with cudgel
穿梭枪	shuttle with spear
刺	piece; stab
刺中	hit the target
点	point; prick
格	parry
弓步劈刺	cut in bow stance

架刀	uphold sabre
架棍	uphold cudgel
架剑	uphold sword
截剑	swing sword obliquely
进步刺剑	step forward and thrust
立剑	standing sword
立舞花棍	rotate cudgel in a vertical circle
撩拳	swing up fist
抡	swing
劈	blow; cut; hit
劈刀	cut with broadsword
劈剑	cut with sword
劈拳	cut with fist
平刺	flat touch
平击	horizontal blow
平抹剑	slice horizontally with sword
扫刀	sweep with broadsword
扫棍	sweep with cudgel
扫剑	sweep with sword
弯弓射虎	Bend Bow to Shoot Tiger
舞花	rotate
斜刺	diagonal stabbing
虚步抡劈剑	cut with arm swing in empty stance
压棍	press cudgel
压剑	press with sword
右带剑	carry sword to the right
右弓步架剑	Parry in Right Bow Step
左弓步架剑	Parry in Left Bow Step
右虚步点剑	Point Sword in Right Empty Stance
斩	chop
直刺	straight thrust

十九、其他词汇 Other Terms

武术	Wushu; martial arts
武术基本功	basic skills of Wushu; Wushu fundamentals
武术术语	Wushu terms
武术教学	Wushu teaching
武术训练	Wushu training
武术课(班)	Wushu class
武术队	Wushu team
武术常用训练法	Wushu general training method
武术分类	Wushu classification
武术套路	Wushu set; Wushu routine
套路结构	structure of set
分段	subsection; section; part; segment
半套	semi-routine
组合	combination
第一段	Section 1
武术健身	physique building of Wushu
武术动作说明与图解	movement explanation and illustration of Wushu
动作名称	movement name
基本方法	basic method
基本动作	basic movement
组合动作	integrated movement
抱拳礼	hold fist salute
精、气、神	essence, breath and spirit
摆幅	amplitude of swing
摆擂台	make open challenges to fights
初级套路	primary routine
传统风格	traditional style
传统套路	traditional routine
喘气	gasp; pant
寸劲	explosive strength

打擂台	take up the challenge to a fight
挡开	fend off
动作	movement
对打	clash; duel; encounter
防守还击	defence and return
刚柔相济	combine hardness and softness
高与肩平	shoulder high; up to the shoulder level
高与腰齐	up to the waist level; waist high
攻防技术	art of attack and defence
功夫	kung fu
规定动作	compulsory movement
规定套路	compulsory routine; required set
过渡动作	transitional movement
基本站立姿势	basic stance
基本姿势	basic position
集体剑	group swordplay
交叉	cross
节奏	rhythm; tempo
精神集中	concentration
静	calmness; quiescence
静止动作	static position
绝招	tour de force
擂台	Wushu arena
连贯	continuity
连续动作	consecutive movement; sequence of movement
灵活	flexibility
慢	slowness
绵绵不断的动作	flowing movement
内功	inner strength
内家功夫	internal school kung fu
外家功夫	external school kung fu
起伏	undulation
气功	breathing control exercise; qigong

CHAPTER 6　WUSHU SPECIFIC WORDS

卡脖子	strangle hold
前脚	front foot; lead foot; leading foot
擒拿	hold and throw
轻	lightness
轻触；轻擦	graze
轻打	bunt
曲线动作	circular motion
拳	fist
拳背	fist-back
拳法	fist position
拳面	fist plane; face of fist
拳面朝上	fist plane facing upward
拳师	boxing coach; pugilist
拳式	boxing form
拳心	hollow of fist
柔和	softness
柔缓的动作	slow and gentle movement
上臂	upper arm
身体竖直	hold torso erect
十八般武艺	various styles of martial arts
实的	solid
收	contraction
穗，缨	tassel
套路布局	routine distribution
套路结构	structure of a set
完成动作	execution
太极推手比赛	Taichi hand-pushing duel
武术对练	Wushu sparring
武术家	martial artist; Wushu expert
武术套路	Wushu routine
武艺	Wushu skills
移	shift
意识	awareness

迎击	meet head-on
硬功	toughening exercise
用力动作	strength part
站立姿势	stance
支撑脚	non-kicking foot; supporting foot
重心转移	shifting of weight
姿势	form; position
自卫	self-defence
中国武术协会	Chinese Wushu Association (CWA)

二十、准备活动　Warm-up Exercise

颈部运动	neck movement
肩部运动	shoulder movement
扩胸运动	chest out movement
体侧运动	body press side movement
体转运动	turn body movement
站桩	stake standing
开步冲拳	Punch Fist in Shoulder-width Stance
马步冲拳	Punch Fist in Horse-ride Step
手型变换	Changes in Hand Forms
仆步抢拍	Swing Arms in Crouch Step
弓步压腿	Press Leg in Bow Step
仆步压腿	Press Leg in Crouch Step
前俯压	press leg forward with bending trunk
正压腿	press leg forward with mouth to toes
侧压腿	press leg at side
纵叉	sidesplit
横叉	cross-splitting
前拍脚	front tap foot
左右抱腿	hold leg on both sides
提膝控腿	raise knee and charge leg
下桥	back bend

涮腰 circle trunk

二十一、放松练习　Relaxing Exercise

顶腰倒立	stand upside down
捶臂叩腿	beat arms and rap legs
拍击放松	tap and relax
拍腹 3 次	tap abdomen 3 times
拍腿 36 次	tap leg 36 times

参 考 文 献

[1] 解守德,李文英.英汉汉英武术常用词汇[M].北京:人民体育出版社,1989.

[2] 刘仕彦等. 汉英——英汉武术气功词汇[M].香港:海峰出版社,1991.

[3] 江百龙等.武术理论基础[M].北京:人民体育出版社,1995.

[4] 蔡仲林,周之华.武术(第三版)[M].北京:高等教育出版社,2015.

[5] 吴必强,许定国.武术基本功[M].重庆:重庆大学出版社,2008.

[6] 吴必强,许定国.套路基础[M].重庆:重庆大学出版社,2008.

[7] 张宗豪,王俪艳,陶玉流.太极英语[M].北京:北京体育大学出版社,2011.